Rubber-Band Banjos and a Java Jive Bass

Projects and Activities on the Science of Music and Sound

Alex Sabbeth

Project illustrations by Laurel Aiello

John Wiley & Sons, Inc.

New York • Chichester • Weinheim • Brisbane • Singapore • Toronto

Library of Congress Cataloging-in-Publication Data
Sabbeth, Alex.
    Rubber-band banjos and a java jive bass : projects and activities
on the science of music and sound / Alex Sabbeth.
        p.   cm.
    Includes index.
    Summary: Presents the science of sound and music, including how
sound is made, how the ear hears sounds, and how different musical
instruments are made.
    ISBN 0–471–15675–2 (pbk. : alk. paper)
    1. Music—Acoustics and physics—Juvenile literature. 2. Sound—
Juvenile literature. 3. Musical instruments—Juvenile literature.
4. Music—Theory, Elementary. [1. Music—Acoustics and physics.
2. Sound. 3. Musical instruments.] I. Title.
ML3805.S2 1997
781—dc20   96–22144

Printed in the United States of America
10 9 8 7 6 5 4 3 2 1

Printed and bound by Malloy Lithographing, Inc.

To young scientists everywhere

Acknowledgments

Long ago, when I was a student, many wonderful people encouraged my interest in science. Walter Stewart, whom I met at Harvard in '66, is the best teacher I ever had.

Frank Firk, Bill Bennet, and Pete Kindlemann were like family during my college years.

Many thanks to Yves Berthelot, for his enthusiasm and help with this book.

Thanks to Uwe Hansen, Austin Caswell, and the Colonel, Bill Lipscomb.

Thanks to Kate Bradford for giving me this opportunity.

Last, thanks to Carol for making it possible.

Contents

Introduction: Tune In!

Welcome to the wonderful world of music and sound! Whether you can play an instrument already or just want to learn a little something about musical science, you'll find a lot of great projects and activities in this book—from making a java jive bass out of a coffee can to conducting your own band in a homemade tux.

Each project is rated for level of difficulty as follows:

One group of notes means an easy project.

Two groups of notes mean a project that will take a little more work.

Three groups of notes mean a project that is a bit more challenging.

And sometimes you will need the help of an adult. If you do, it will be clearly marked in that activity.

In chapter 1, you'll do some experiments to find out how sounds are made and how you hear them. You'll also get to play musical glasses and learn some interesting facts about animal hearing.

In chapters 2 to 4, you'll discover the three main categories of instruments: strings (including guitars, violins, and even pianos), winds (including saxophones, flutes, and trumpets), and percussion (including drums, xylophones, and chimes). You'll make a banjo and a fiddle, an oboe and a flute, a drum and a tambourine. You'll learn about how the thickness of a string or the tightness of a drumhead affects sound. And you'll meet some very musical scientists, such as Alexander Graham Bell (piano) and Richard Feynman (bongo drums).

In chapters 5 and 6, you'll see how the electronic age has changed the world of music by providing new ways to create and record sounds. You'll put together your own electronic studio and learn how you can "see" a sound.

In chapters 7 and 8, you'll learn the basics of reading music and conducting an orchestra. Start with some cool rhythm games, then put on your conductor's tux and grab a baton. Let the music begin!

Sound and Hearing

What sounds do you hear every day? Your own voice? Your dog barking? A phone ringing? In one day you will hear hundreds of sounds. You make some of them yourself by talking and singing, clapping your hands, or by zipping up and down the sidewalk on skates. Sounds are made by machines, such as computers and vacuum cleaners. Other sounds just happen naturally, like the sound of rain falling on a roof, or a bird singing.

Sound and Movement

What do all these different sounds have in common? They are all caused by movement.

It's easy to see your hands move when you clap them. But what do you think moves when you sing or talk? It's your vocal cords. They vibrate every time you say something.

Try moving absolutely silently. Do you know of anything that can move without a sound? Even the "silent" owl makes a slight sound as it glides and pounces on its prey.

Sound and Vibrations

Vibration is a rapid movement that repeats itself. A bell, a stereo speaker, and even your vocal cords all vibrate, causing sound. Slow vibrations make low sounds, and fast ones make high sounds.

Tapping or striking an object makes it vibrate. You hear a bell when it's struck by its clapper. The ringing sound depends on the bell's size and weight.

The Amazing Owl

An owl can fly almost silently because of the special design of its wings. Feathers are placed so that even when flapping, the wings create almost no sound. This allows the owl to hunt without alerting its prey.

Barn owls also have extra-sensitive hearing, thanks to the special shape of their face. The area around the eyes acts like a funnel. It collects sound, so the owl can hear the faintest rustle of leaves or a bird's chirping.

Vibrating Voices

Can you feel your voice making sound?

What to Do

Try touching your throat while you talk. Can you feel the vibrations? Now try singing as low as your voice will go. Can you feel the slower vibrations? Now try singing as high as you can. What changed?

What You Discovered

You could easily feel your throat vibrating when you sang really low. The vibrations were harder to feel when you sang high.

Why?

Low sounds are caused by slow vibrations, which you can easily feel. High sounds are produced by faster, usually smaller, movements that are harder to feel.

Now Try This

Look at the strings while you play a guitar. Pluck the lowest-sounding string and watch it vibrate. Now pluck the highest-sounding string. It's almost impossible to see it vibrate, because it moves so much faster. A guitar string must vibrate at least 20 times per second to produce a sound you can hear. Even at this speed, a vibrating string sounds too low for most people to hear it.

Good Vibrations Boogie-Band Harmonica

♪ *Here's an instrument you can make that shows how vibration works to create sound. You'll feel the vibrations as they tickle your lips. Make several harmonicas and have a vibrating boogie jam with your friends.*

What You'll Need

small comb
4-inch (10-cm)-square piece of
  waxed paper

What to Do

1 Fold the waxed paper in half and insert the comb inside the paper.

2 To play your instrument, press your lips lightly against the paper and sing *dos* and *das*. Move the comb back and forth to make different sounds. The louder your voice, the more the paper will vibrate.

Water Music

♪ *Water-glass music has been around for centuries. This simple instrument not only sounds beautiful but also demonstrates how vibration works in a water glass.*

What You'll Need

several water glasses

water

food coloring

spoon

ribbons, beads, or braided yarn

What to Do

1 Fill the glasses to different levels. Add food coloring to each for pizzazz.

2 Decorate the spoon with brightly colored ribbons, beads, or braided yarn.

3 To play your instrument, lightly tap the glasses with the spoon. Experiment with different amounts of water. Adding water slows down the vibrations of the glass. This makes a lower sound.

Let's Play

♫ Here's how you can play a well-known song on the water glasses. By changing the level of water, you change the pitch of each glass's sound. **Pitch** is the highness or lowness of a sound.

Because glasses differ, you may need to experiment with water levels if the song doesn't sound quite right.

What You'll Need

6 tall water glasses of about the same style

water

ruler

scissors

paper

pencil

spoon

What to Do

1 Fill each glass as follows, measuring from the bottom of the glass:

Glass 1 5¾ inches (14.4 cm)
Glass 2 5½ inches (13.75 cm)
Glass 3 4¾ inches (11.9 cm)
Glass 4 4½ inches (11.25 cm)
Glass 5 3¾ inches (9.4 cm)
Glass 6 3¼ inches (8.1 cm)

2 Place the glasses in a row with glass 1 on the left. Water levels will be lower as you move toward the right.

3 Cut 6 small pieces of paper. Write one number on each piece, 1 through 6. Place each piece of paper in front of the glass given that number.

4 To play "Twinkle, Twinkle, Little Star," tap the glasses, following the numbers as shown.

1-1-5-5-6-6-5 Twinkle, Twinkle, little star,
4-4-3-3-2-2-1 How I wonder what you are!
5-5-4-4-3-3-2 Up above the world so high,
5-5-4-4-3-3-2 Like a diamond in the sky.

1-1-5-5-6-6-5 Twinkle, Twinkle, little star,
4-4-3-3-2-2-1 How I wonder what you are!

Glass Harmonica

♪ *This heavenly-sounding instrument is a simple version of Franklin's invention.*

What You'll Need

several stemmed drinking glasses
water

What to Do

1. Fill each glass with a different amount of water.

2. To play, moisten your finger and rub it evenly around the top of each glass to make a ringing sound. *NOTE: Your fingers must be clean and oil-free.*

Rubbing an object causes it to vibrate. When you scratch your fingernail across a desk, the nail and desktop vibrate, causing sound. Violins and cellos work the same way. The bow hairs rub on the strings, causing them to vibrate.

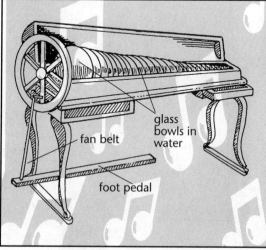

fan belt
glass bowls in water
foot pedal

BENJAMIN FRANKLIN (1706–1790) was good at everything he tried. He owned a newspaper business, published *Poor Richard's Almanack*, and was a famous diplomat. While living in London, he entertained friends by playing tunes on the violin, guitar, and harp. He even designed a version of a musical instrument called the glass harmonica. Franklin's instrument consisted of a row of glass bowls mounted on a long axle attached to a wheel. The lower half of these bowls rested in water, so their rims were always wet. The instrument was played by pressing a foot pedal that turned the axle. The player used the fingers of both hands to rub the wet glasses as they turned. This created vibrations that made a ringing sound. The glass harmonica was very popular in Europe, and great musicians such as Mozart wrote charming pieces for it. People loved the soft ringing of Franklin's lovely invention.

How Things Sound

How do different types of objects sound?

What You'll Need

large, soft eraser
sharpened pencil
objects of varying hardness,
    such as metal ruler,
    metal pot lid,
    drinking glass,
    shoe, and
    book
string

What To Do

1 Stick the eraser on the point of the pencil.

2 Tie enough string around each object (except the glass or any other breakable object) so that you can hang it.

3 Hold up each object in turn by its string and tap it with the eraser.

4 Try tapping other objects around the house (ignoring temptations like your mom's crystal or your brother's model train).

What You Discovered

The objects made different sounds. Hard, stiff things made louder sounds than soft, bendable ones.

Why?

Soft things yield, absorbing (soaking up) the energy from the striker. Harder objects absorb less energy.

Electromagnetic Sound

· · · ·

A more mysterious way to make sound is with an **electromagnet** (a wire coil that becomes a magnet when electricity flows through it). The speaker in your stereo makes sound because of a small electromagnet inside. The flow of electricity from the amplifier passes through the electromagnet, causing the speaker to vibrate and produce musical sounds.

Sound and Air

Air is also important to sound. Sound is caused by movement, but it needs air to travel to your ears. If you were on the moon without a space helmet, you wouldn't hear anything because there's no air on the moon.

Air not only transmits sounds but also can make sound. A dramatic example is thunder. During a storm, air can be heated by lightning, a giant electrical spark jumping between the clouds and the earth. The rapidly heated air makes a loud boom, which we know as thunder.

The Sound of Two Hands Clapping

How does clapping make sound?

What to Do

Clap your hands so that your palms cross like an X. Then try clapping backward so that the backs of your hands hit each other. Which way makes more sound?

What You Discovered

When you clap your hands the first way, with the palms crossed, the sound is louder than when you clap your hands back to back.

Why?

When you clap with your palms together, air is momentarily trapped. The trapped air is compressed (squeezed together). When it escapes, it expands (spreads out) quickly, causing the loud bang. This is what happens when a balloon breaks.

The Speed of Sound

Which is faster, thunder or lightning?

What to Do

During a storm, count slowly as soon as you see a lightning flash. Count like this: one Mississippi, two Mississippi, and so on until you hear the thunder. Each count represents 1 second.

What You Discovered

If you counted to five, it took sound 5 seconds to reach you, long after you saw the flash.

Why?

The lightning is one mile away. Sound travels through air about ⅕ mile (0.3 km) per second. Light travels about a million times faster.

Sound and Waves

How do we hear sound through the air? How does the vibrating object affect our ears so we hear it? The answer is that the air around the object vibrates also. The guitar string vibrates against the air around it. That sets the air in motion, with vibrations traveling out in all directions. Listeners far away can hear the guitar because of vibrating air. The sound travels through the air in **waves** (regular movements that repeat themselves).

Have you ever zoomed on ocean waves with a boogie board or raft? If you have, you know that waves can travel. Sound waves travel through air and many other materials as well. Sound actually travels better through solids than through air. It takes 5 seconds for sound to travel 1 mile (1.6 km) in air. Sound goes five times faster in water, and also seems louder. Sound travels fastest, and seems loudest, in solids like metal or rock.

Think about when you throw a rock into the water of a lake or pond. Ripples form from the splash, traveling out in bigger and bigger circles. Sound waves behave just like these ripples. They begin at a source and spread out in all directions. They travel a great distance before they fade away.

 **Scientist's Corner** **Sounds in Solids**

How does sound heard in the air compare to sound heard through a solid?

What to Do

1 Scratch your fingernail across a tabletop as softly as possible, so you can barely hear it.

2 Do the same thing while listening with your ear pressed against the tabletop.

What you Discovered

The scratching sounded louder when you listened with your ear pressed against the table.

Why?

Most of the sound waves travel within the table instead of spreading out into the air. Listening through the air, you're missing most of the sound. Sound also travels more quickly in solids than through air. Solids, gases like air, and liquids are all made up of tiny particles called molecules. The molecules are packed closer together in solids, so vibrations can travel faster from one molecule to the next.

What is an echo?

What You'll Need

jump rope
helper

What to Do

1 Hold one end of the jump rope, and have your helper hold the other end. Stand with the rope stretched taut.

2 While your helper holds his end of the rope still, quickly jerk your end once.

What You Discovered

You created a wave that ran from one end of the rope to the other, then bounced back.

Why?

Different kinds of waves can reflect (bounce off) an object. Reflection of sound waves is called an echo.

Sound Navigation

Dolphins can locate objects easily even when blindfolded. They use high whistles and clicks to "see" underwater by studying the returning echoes. Dolphins aren't the only animals that can "see" with sound. In the darkest night, bats are able to zoom through dense forests in pursuit of insects. People also use sound. Submarines send sound signals to measure how far below the surface they are and how deep the sea is. Researchers reflect sound off the ocean floor, measuring mountains and valleys deep underwater.

What is a compression wave?

What You'll Need

Slinky

What to Do

1 Position the Slinky on its side between your hands on a table, then stretch it slightly.

2 Keeping your left hand still, quickly jerk the Slinky with your right hand.

3 Watch the wave go from your right hand to your left, then back again.

What You Discovered

You created another type of wave that made an echo. It's called a **compression wave**. A compression wave happens when the molecules of a material are alternately compressed and expanded. It is found inside wind instruments, like the clarinet, when they are played.

Frequency

Waves are measured by their **frequency**. Sound waves can be spaced closer together or farther apart. Closely spaced waves go by more often, so they have higher frequency. High-frequency sounds have higher pitch than low-frequency sounds.

Look at the two trains illustrated here. The passenger cars in train 1 are smaller than those in train 2. Both trains are traveling down the track at the same speed. But because the cars of train 1 are smaller, more of them will pass the signpost than those in train 2. In scientific terms, these smaller cars have a higher frequency, because more of them will pass by.

Sound and Hearing

Sound travels by means of vibrations (waves) in a material like air or water. When the vibrations from the air (or other material) reach your ear, they pass into the ear through a funnel-shaped passage called the ear canal. The ear canal focuses the sound onto the eardrum (a tiny drumlike membrane between the outer ear and inner ear). The eardrum vibrates along with the vibrations of the incoming air. The eardrum moves only slightly, even with a very loud sound.

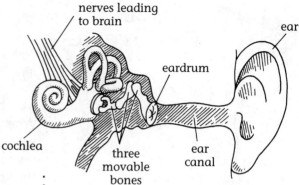

nerves leading to brain

ear

eardrum

cochlea

three movable bones

ear canal

Three bones move along with the eardrum. These bones push into the **cochlea** (a coiled tube in the inner ear which is filled with fluid), wiggling a tiny membrane inside. These movements are converted to electrical pulses, which are passed to nerves (fibers that send messages to and from the brain). These pulses include information about pitch and how loud the sound is. Amazingly, you can identify sounds from these pulses.

Telephones work just about the same way. The motions of a small plate inside the mouthpiece are converted to electrical pulses that are sent out over telephone lines.

Direction of Sound

How do we know where a sound comes from? Two features help us out. The first is the shape of our ears, which helps us locate some sounds, mostly high-frequency ones. The modified funnel shape emphasizes sounds to our sides, but minimizes sounds in front and back of us. This is less noticeable with low-frequency sounds. They tend to spread out, so it's hard to know where they're coming from.

The second is the fact that we have two ears. If we hear something on our left, our left ear will register a louder sound than our right ear. This and other slight differences give us a good idea of a sound's location.

Ear-ee Discoveries

Are two ears better than one?

What You'll Need

blindfold

cotton ball

butter knife

spoon

large, empty, plastic trash can

helper

NOTE: This experiment requires a large room with plenty of furniture.

What to Do

1 Put on the blindfold, then carefully put the cotton ball in one ear.

2 Have a helper tap the knife with the spoon while she stands in different parts of the room. Try to point to your helper's location.

3 Have your helper turn over the trash can and tap the top with the spoon, making the lowest possible sound. Try again to point to her location.

4 Now take out the cotton ball and repeat steps 2 and 3. Try again to point to your helper's location.

What You Discovered

When you had the cotton in one ear, it was very hard to know where your helper was. When you took the cotton out, it was easier to locate her. You may have noticed that the higher-pitched sound of the spoon and knife was easier to locate than the lower-pitched sound of the spoon and trash can.

Why?

Having two ears helps you figure out what direction a sound is coming from. Your brain compares the loudness of the sound heard by each ear. The sound appears to come from the direction in which it is loudest. Echoes in the room can weaken this effect, though. Higher-pitched sounds tend to travel in a straight line, without spreading out like low-pitched sounds. This makes it easier to tell where they come from.

Our hearing has certain limitations. We can't hear very high- or low-frequency sounds as easily as sounds in the middle of our hearing range. As we grow older, we lose more sensitivity to high-frequency sounds. In addition to this natural loss, our hearing can be damaged by very loud sounds. Have you ever noticed ringing in your ears? That's a normal reaction to very loud sounds. If it doesn't go away, it might mean permanent hearing loss.

It's important to protect our ears from loud sounds both at work and play. You'll see highway and airport workers using ear covers. Even musicians have to be careful. Loud bass guitars, trumpets, and percussion instruments can all cause hearing problems.

Animal Hearing

Animals such as dogs and cats can turn their ears around to accurately locate sounds. Some animals can hear sounds that are too low- or high-pitched for us to hear. Bats emit very high-pitched sounds, and steer through darkness using the echoes. Dogs and cats also hear sounds too high for us. Elephants can communicate using sounds too low for us to hear, but strong enough for us to feel (like a bass guitar in a loud rock band). They can hear each other from miles (kilometers) away, listening with their huge ears held open.

Hearing without Ears!

You hear because your eardrum vibrates along with waves traveling in the air. Some animals can hear without ears. Snakes don't have visible ears, and they hear through the air poorly. They can feel vibrations in the ground, which helps them find food and avoid danger.

Vibrations in the ground travel through the snake's bones to its brain. Part of our hearing works the same way. When you speak, sing, or eat, you hear sound in two ways. Some of the sound that comes from inside your head reaches your inner ear by traveling through your bones. This is called **bone conduction.** The rest of the sound travels in the air and reaches your inner ear through your eardrum. The sound heard by bone conduction is missing when you hear a recording of your voice. You hear it only through the air. That's why some people say they can't recognize their own voice on an answering machine.

How do snakes "hear"?

What You'll Need
stereo system with good speakers

What To Do

1. Play your favorite music on your stereo. The volume doesn't have to be very loud.

2. Stand very still in front of the speakers. Breathe slowly and relax. What do you feel?

What You Discovered
You felt a buzzing inside your head and chest.

Why?
Your body has large **cavities** (hollow spaces), just like a guitar or drum. The air in these spaces vibrates along with the sounds around them. A drum's cavity **amplifies** (makes louder) the sound of the drumhead when it's struck. You can feel your chest cavity vibrating along with the music.

Even if you didn't have ears, you'd notice these vibrations, just like the snake. Many deaf people love to dance. They feel the music in their bodies and enjoy dancing along with its vibrations.

Ventriloquist Birds

Ventriloquists are people who can "throw" their voice—that is, make it seem as if it's coming from somewhere else. Some small birds, like the chaffinch, can also "throw" their voices to warn other birds of danger. They use a high, drawn-out call that seems to come from nowhere—or everywhere. Researchers believe this call confuses predators by making them unable to tell where it's coming from.

What musical sounds can be found in nature?

What to Do

1. Go outside to a quiet place, away from traffic noise. Maybe take a walk through a park or pasture, or along a quiet beach. *CAUTION: For safety's sake, do not walk alone. Have an adult with you.*

2 Listen to all the sounds you hear. Which instruments does Nature use in her orchestra? You might hear leaves rustling, birds chirping, water gurgling, or waves crashing.

3 While on your outing, try to find the most unusual, or softest, or prettiest sounds.

What You Discovered

You probably heard many sounds that could be used in music. Many musicians try to imitate the sounds of nature. In all kinds of music, you can hear imitations of natural sounds. Thunderstorms, murmuring mountain streams, and galloping horses are just a few of the sounds we can hear imitated in music.

Now try this

Match these natural sounds with a musical instrument that might sound like them.

Duck quacking   Tambourine shaking

Bird singing   Oboe

Thunder   Flute

Waves crashing   Wood block

Horse trotting   Cymbals

Water splashing   Drums

Oboe
Flute
Cymbals
Drums
Wood block
Tambourine shaking

Duck quacking
Bird singing
Thunder
Waves crashing
Horse trotting
Water splashing

Answer

Dolphins and Whales Communicate
• • • •

Have you heard of singing whales? You can find recordings of their "songs" in many gift shops. Marine mammals use sound to communicate. Dolphins appear to use whistles and clicks in their "conversations." Because sound travels so quickly underwater, even widely separated dolphins can be "in touch." Researchers hope to solve the mystery of their "conversations" and learn more about these intelligent creatures.

2 Stringed Instruments

So many musical instruments use strings—guitars, violins, banjos. Even you use a kind of string, called vocal cords, when you talk and sing. Most stringed instruments have a few basic parts in common. There is a hollow body, usually with an opening in one side. Attached to the body is a long neck, which consists mainly of the fingerboard. The strings are attached to one end of the neck by pegs, then run along the fingerboard, over the opening in the body, to a small support called the bridge, which keeps the strings in place. The pegs at the end of the neck are turned to change the tension (tautness) of the strings. This is called "tuning" the strings.

Stringed instruments are played by pressing the fingers down on the strings. This changes the strings' length, causing them to vibrate at different frequencies and thus to make different sounds. Shortening a string makes it sound higher. Many stringed instruments have frets set into their neck. These are metal ridges that show the player where to put his fingers. This makes it easier to play each pitch accurately, or "in tune."

Strings used to be made of animal fibers. Today, strings are usually made of man-made fibers or metal. Some expensive strings are still made of animal fibers. Although these strings might sound better than those of man-made materials, they wear out more quickly.

Strings produce different sounds depending on their length and thickness. The short strings of a violin make a higher sound than the long strings of a guitar. It's easy to see the different thicknesses of guitar strings. Tightening a string also changes the way it sounds.

Vocal Frogs

Vocal cords work great for humans. What other animals do you think have them? The frog was the first animal we know of to use vocal cords. They croak choruses and solos, whether they are looking for mates or defending their territory.

Thick and Thin Strings

Scientist's Corner

How does thickness affect a string's sound?

What You'll Need

pencil
ruler
18-by-6-by-1-inch (45-by-15-by-2.5-cm) board (cut to size at a lumber store or by an adult)
3 size 14 screw eyes
3 feet (0.9 m) each of 50-, 30-, and 5-pound-test fishing line (available in a sporting goods store)
3 plastic ½ gallon (1.9-liter) jugs with handles
measuring cup
water

What to Do

1 With the pencil, draw a line across the board 1 inch (2.5 cm) from one end.

2 Screw 1 screw eye into the center of the line. Screw each of the other screw eyes 2 inches

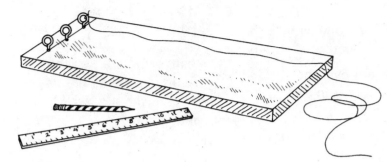

(5 cm) away on either side of the first screw eye.

3 Tie a piece of fishing line to each screw eye.

4 Place the board on the edge of a table so that the end opposite the screw eyes is even with the edge of the table.

5 Let the ends of the fishing line fall over the table edge.

6 Tie a plastic jug by the handle to the end of each fishing line.

7 Fill each jug with 2 cups (500 ml) of water.

8 Adjust the jugs so that they hang from the end of the board over the table edge. Make sure the fishing lines are straight

from the screw eyes to the end of the board.

9 Pluck each line, then compare the sounds.

What You Discovered

The sound of each line depends on its thickness. The 50-pound fishing line sounded lower than the 30-pound, which sounded lower than the 5-pound.

Why?

Thick strings are like a loaded truck compared to an empty one. With so much weight to move, they naturally go slower. If the length and tension are the same, thick strings will always vibrate slower and sound lower than thin strings.

Stretched Strings

How does tension affect a string's sound?

What You'll Need

board with screw eyes from the previous experiment

two 3-foot (0.9 m) pieces of 50-pound-test fishing line

3 plastic 1/2-gallon (1.9-liter) jugs with handles

measuring cup

water

What to Do

1. Remove the 30- and 5-pound pieces of fishing line from the board.

2. Replace the removed fishing lines with the two 50-pound pieces of fishing line.

3. Place the wood board on the edge of the table.

4. Tie a jug to each line.

5. Fill one jug with 2 cups (500 ml) of water, one with 3 cups (750 ml) of water, and one with 5 cups (1,250 ml) of water.

6. Arrange the jugs over the edge of the table as in the previous experiment.

7. Pluck each line, and describe the sounds you hear.

What You Discovered

The line attached to the heaviest jug sounded highest. The lightest jug sounded lowest.

Why?

Increasing the weight stretches the line tighter. This increases the tension. The tighter the string, the higher the sound. A tighter string springs back to its original position faster than a loose string. By springing back more quickly, the string produces sounds that have a higher frequency and higher pitch. Stringed instruments are tuned by changing the tension of their strings.

Pedal Play

The harp's strings are adjusted by pedals. The player has to push them with her feet while playing.

Long and Short Strings

How does length affect a string's sound?

What You'll Need

board setup from the previous experiment

What to Do

Press a string down with one finger, and pluck it with another. Then press it at a different point and pluck it again. How does the sound change?

What You Discovered

When your finger shortens the string's length, a higher sound results. Lengthening the string makes it sound lower.

Why?

When you pluck a string, it takes time for it to start vibrating. Because the vibrations have farther to go, they take longer to travel through a long string than a short one. This makes the long string vibrate slower, producing a lower pitch.

Most stringed instruments have a hollow body. The strings are stretched over an opening in the body. When they vibrate, they cause the air inside the body to vibrate also. This reinforces (strengthens) the sound of the strings.

Scientist's Corner

Musical Shoe Box

Why does a guitar have a hollow body?

What You'll Need

pencil
ruler
shoe box with lid
scissors
large rubber band

What to Do

1 Draw a 1-by-5-inch (2.5-by-12.5-cm) rectangle in the middle of the lid of the shoe box as shown.

2 Use the scissors to cut out the rectangle.

3 Stretch the rubber band around your fingers and pluck it. Notice the sound quality.

4 Put the lid on the box. Stretch the rubber band all the way around the box so that it is over the opening in the lid.

5 Pluck the rubber band again and notice the difference of the sound quality.

What You Discovered

The rubber band makes a much stronger sound when it's stretched around the box.

Why?

When the rubber band is plucked, the air around it starts to vibrate along with it. The sound waves (vibrations) travel away and fade. The box serves the same purpose as the hollow body of a guitar or violin. It reinforces the sound by keeping the waves from traveling away.

Some instruments, like the violin and cello, use a small device called a **mute** to soften the sound. The player attaches the mute to the top of the bridge.

Scientist's Corner
Quiet Clothespin

How does a mute work?

What You'll Need

large rubber band

empty 2-pound (0.9-kg) coffee can with plastic lid

1-inch (2.5-cm)-square piece of corrugated cardboard

spring-type clothespin

What to Do

1 Stretch the rubber band around the can from top to bottom.

2 Place the cardboard under the rubber band so that it is at a right angle to the lid.

3 Pluck the rubber band and notice the sound it makes.

4 Clip the clothespin onto the cardboard as shown.

5 Pluck the rubber band and notice how the sound changes.

What You Discovered

The sound was softer after you added the clothespin.

Why?

The weight of the clothespin limited the cardboard's vibrations, making the sound softer.

Guitar

The guitar is the most versatile instrument you can find. It can play classical music written hundreds of years ago, or be strummed to accompany folksingers, or rock with the Beatles and Pearl Jam. On the prairies, it was a favorite guest around campfires when cowboys rested after herding their cattle. Elvis played and sang as he rocked and rolled for his adoring fans. Some rock bands got caught up with excitement and smashed a few innocent guitars.

The guitar stems from the *vihuela*, a stringed instrument played in sixteenth-century Spain. Early guitars had four or five sets of double strings—two strings set close together and tuned the same way. Double strings probably made a louder sound than a single string. Guitars were often elaborately decorated with inlaid wood, so they looked as beautiful as they sounded. By 1800, versions resembling today's **acoustic** (not electrically amplified) models were used in Europe. They had metal frets set into the fingerboard.

In 1935 a new sound was created when the first guitar was amplified. Amplified, or electric, guitars sound very different from acoustic models. An electric guitar's sound depends on speakers and amplifiers. The acoustic guitar's tone is the result of wood quality and shape.

The guitar is usually played by plucking the strings over the body with the fingers of one hand while pressing the strings against the fingerboard with the other hand. A pick (a small, thin piece of plastic or metal) can be used to pluck. Plucking is used to play a **melody** (several pitches sounded one after the other as a tune). Strumming several strings produces **chords** (three or more pitches sounded at the same time). Chords can be played to accompany the melody.

Flashing Hands

For special effects, the guitar's body can be slapped. Spanish **flamenco** music features rhythmic tapping of the guitar's body to accompany a dancer. The flashing hands of one player earned him the nickname "Manitas de Plata," or Little Silver Hands.

Shoe-Box Guitar

🎵 *Guitars are played by plucking and strumming the strings and even tapping a beat on the body of the guitar. Try all these techniques with your shoe-box guitar.*

What You'll Need

scissors

ruler

shoe box with lid

white glue

4 toothpicks

4 large rubber bands of various thickness

pencil

What to Do

1 Cut a hole about 3 inches (7.5 cm) square near one end of the shoe-box lid.

2 Glue the toothpicks onto the lid of the box, spacing them evenly between the hole and the opposite end of the lid, as shown. These are the frets.

3 Place the lid on the box. Slide the rubber bands, from thickest to thinnest, around the box and lid so that they go across the hole.

4 Insert the pencil under the rubber bands at the end near the hole. This is the bridge.

5 Play the guitar by plucking the rubber bands. Try making different sounds by holding down the rubber bands at the frets while plucking. Notice that the thicker rubber bands create a lower sound.

STEPS 1 AND 2

STEP 4

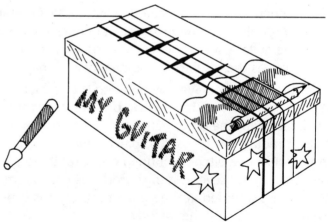

Banjo

The banjo is an American invention heard mainly in folk music and jazz. In a concert, the banjo player usually gets a chance to play a dazzling solo, full of fast-moving variations of the main tune. It can seem as though two or three banjos are playing at once.

The banjo has frets like a guitar, and four or five strings. Its body is really a small, round drum that can be slapped while the player plucks the strings. Beautiful woods can be used, making the banjo as beautiful as a guitar. The drumhead can be decorated with designs.

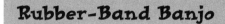

Rubber-Band Banjo

Many banjo players decorate the drumhead, or vellum, as you will do in this rubber-band banjo.

What You'll Need

many colors of acrylic paint

paintbrush

empty 12-ounce (340-g) plastic tub with lid from whipped topping

18-by-1-by-¼-inch (45-by-2.5-by-0.6-cm) wood slat

marking pen

scissors

ruler

2 large, long rubber bands of different thickness

masking tape

2-by-1-inch (5-by-2.5-cm) piece of cardboard

What to Do

1 Paint decorations on the tub's lid and outer sides. Let the paint dry thoroughly.

STEP 1

2 Place the slat across the center of the open tub. On the rim of the tub, mark the four places where the edges of the slat touch the rim.

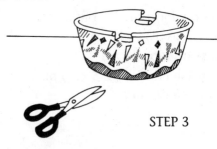

STEP 3

3 Using your marks as a guide, cut ½-inch (1.25-cm) slits in each side of the tub. Fold the flaps inward.

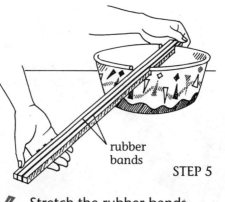

rubber bands

STEP 5

4 Stretch the rubber bands around the length of the slat.

5 Place the slat in the notches of the tub so that the slat extends 1 inch (2.5 cm) past one side of the tub.

6 Slide the lid onto the tub so that it goes over the slat and under the rubber bands.

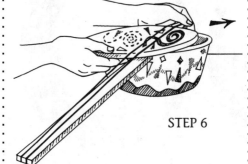

STEP 6

7 Secure the lid to the tub's sides with tape.

8 Fold the piece of cardboard in half so that it measures 1 inch (2.5 cm) square.

9 Cut two ¼-inch (0.6-cm) slots in the folded edge of the cardboard. Space the slots about ½ inch (1.25 cm) apart, centered on the cardboard.

STEPS 7–10

10 Holding the cardboard with the slots faceup, insert it between the rubber bands and lid, as shown. Insert each rubber band in a slot, then secure the cardboard to the lid with tape.

11 Play the banjo by plucking or strumming the rubber bands with your right hand while pressing them down along the wood slat with your left hand.

Violin

A famous violin teacher once said, "You can't really own your violin. After years of practicing so hard, it really owns you!"

The modern violin has its roots in Italy. You may have heard the name Stradivarius. Antonio Stradivari (1644?–1737) perfected earlier versions of the violin. The whole world now treasures his violins. A violin built by "Strad" can cost $3 million.

The violin has a beautiful, sweet tone. It shares the guitar's figure-eight shape, but it is smaller. From end to end, it measures about 22 inches (55 cm). The front of the body, just under the strings, is made of softwood, like spruce. The back must be of hardwood, like maple, to support the pressure of the four strings. Just underneath the bridge, inside the violin, is a peg called the sound post, which also supports the strings' pressure. The position of the sound post affects the violin's tone. Because there are no frets set into the fingerboard, the violinist must know exactly where to put his fingers to play "in tune." Most students work hardest to learn this.

The violin is played by drawing a bow (a wooden stick with horsehairs stretched from end to end) across the strings with the right hand while pressing the strings against the fingerboard with the left hand. Bowing properly can be very difficult. Some players think this is the hardest thing about playing a violin. The bow's back-and-forth movement over the strings should be very smooth, in contrast to the pressing and lifting of the fingers on the strings. Sometimes players pluck the strings rather than bow them. This is called playing **pizzicato**.

The violin is a melodic instrument, which means it usually plays one pitch at a time. Bowing lets the violinist play more than one string at once. Chords can be bowed or plucked. The viola and cello are larger versions of the violin. The viola sounds lower than the violin, and the cello sounds lower still.

What Makes a Strad Sound So Good?

Scientists have struggled to understand what makes a Stradivarius sound so good. Many theories have been suggested. Some researchers think it has to do with the exact shape and thickness of each piece of wood. Others emphasize the varnish. Some think the violins got better as they aged, because frequent playing made their tone more mellow. One theory is that the violins sound better because their wood was soaked in briny water for months. Minerals and salts soaked into the wood, altering its fibers. The difference can be seen under a powerful microscope.

Today's violin has changed slightly from earlier versions. Its neck is longer, and the strings are pulled tighter, giving a higher pitch to the whole instrument. This gives a richer and louder sound. Strings can be made of metal instead of animal fiber. These strings are easier to use because they don't break as easily. The best strings are made of animal fiber wound with fine silver or aluminum wire.

These minor improvements only add to the violin's greatness. No scientific advance has been able to produce violins equal to the great models built in the 1700s. Here, science has not improved quality or lowered cost. Violins today are made using the same basic procedures of centuries ago.

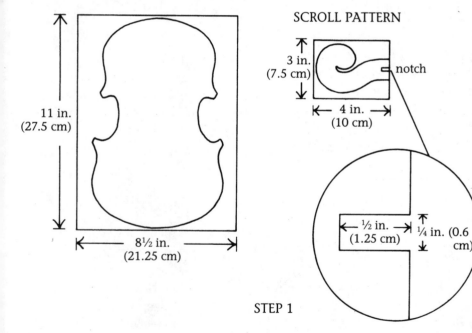

VIOLIN BODY PATTERN

11 in. (27.5 cm)

8½ in. (21.25 cm)

SCROLL PATTERN

3 in. (7.5 cm)

notch

4 in. (10 cm)

½ in. (1.25 cm)

¼ in. (0.6 cm)

STEP 1

Country Fiddle

"Fiddle" is a playful name for the violin, especially when the instrument is played in folk or country music. No matter what kind of music you like, this project will get you fiddling up a storm. Pluck it with your fingers, or play it with the bow you'll make in the next project.

What You'll Need

pencil

8½-by-11-inch (21.25-by-27.5-cm) piece of corrugated cardboard

3-by-4-inch (7.5-by-10-cm) piece of corrugated cardboard

scissors

ruler

white glue

18-by-1-by-¼-inch (45-by-2.5-by-0.6-cm) wood slat

brown tempera paint

paintbrush

black felt-tipped marker

8 size 214½ screw eyes

4 size 14 screw eyes

fishing line: 50, 30, 10, and 5 lb. test - 3 feet (0.9 m) each

What to Do

1 Use the pencil to draw the shape of the violin body on the larger piece of cardboard. Draw the shape of the violin scroll on the smaller piece of cardboard. Your patterns should be 4 times larger than the ones shown here.

2 Cut out the scroll and body.

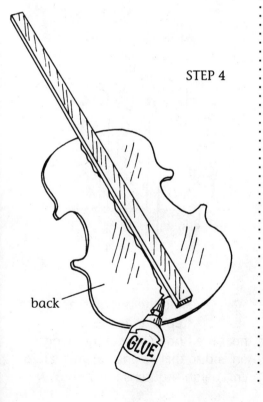

STEP 4

back

3 Cut a 1-by-½-inch (2.5-by-1.25-cm) rectangle from the scraps and set it aside. This will be used later as the violin's bridge.

4 Make the neck by gluing the slat to the center of the body, starting about 1 inch (2.5 cm) from the wide end of the body and running the length of the body. This side of the body is the back.

STEP 5

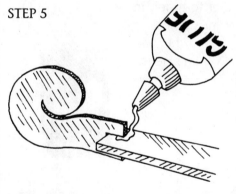

5 Turn the violin over to the front side. Apply glue to the slot in the scroll. Slide the scroll onto the free end of the neck, centering the scroll as shown.

6 Paint the entire violin brown. Let the paint dry.

STEP 7

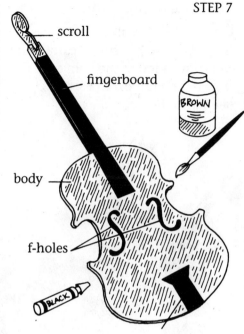

scroll

fingerboard

body

f-holes

tail piece

7 Add detail to the violin with the marker. Draw the tailpiece, f-holes, and fingerboard, as shown.

8 With the body faceup, use 4 of the smaller screw eyes (size 214½) to pierce the cardboard along the edge of the tailpiece, as shown. Then screw the screw eyes deep into the slat.

10 Screw 2 large screw eyes (size 14) into each side of the neck at the top. Do not tighten them into the wood; leave one-fourth of each screw out of the wood so that it can be turned later to tune the strings. These are the violin's pegs.

13 Pull the free end of each string tightly around the base of the small screw eye in the neck, then wrap it around the nearest large screw several times. Thread it through the large eye, then make several knots in the string.

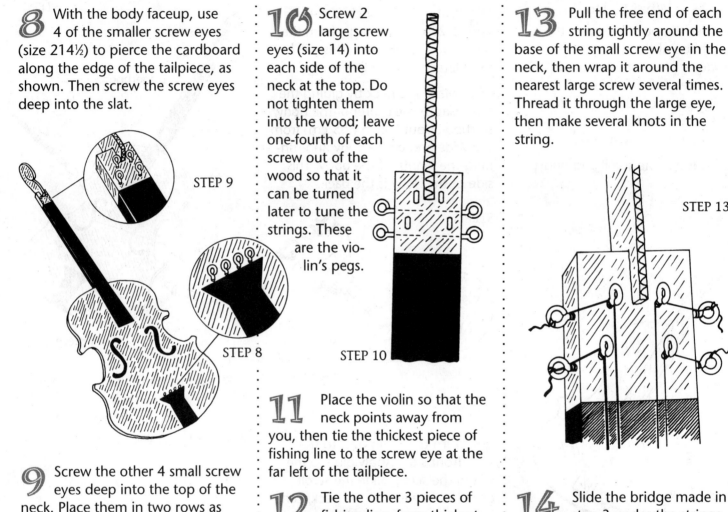

STEP 9

STEP 8

STEP 10

STEP 13

9 Screw the other 4 small screw eyes deep into the top of the neck. Place them in two rows as shown, with the 2 inner screws at the top of the neck and the 2 outer screws below them.

11 Place the violin so that the neck points away from you, then tie the thickest piece of fishing line to the screw eye at the far left of the tailpiece.

12 Tie the other 3 pieces of fishing line, from thickest to thinnest, around the other 3 screw eyes of the tailpiece. These are the strings.

14 Slide the bridge made in step 3 under the strings near the f-holes. Stand the bridge on end so that its one-half-inch (1.25 cm) height tightens the strings.

15 Gently tighten the large screw eyes to "tune" the strings.

16 To play, hold the neck of the violin in your left hand and put the other end on your left shoulder with your chin resting on it. Use the fingers of your left hand to press the strings against the fingerboard, while plucking the strings pizzicato with your right hand.

Violin Bow

♪ *If you want to try playing your violin with a bow, you can make one from a branch of a tree. Rosin, available in a music store, is a crumbly substance made from the deadwood of pine trees and used on the hairs (you'll use thread). It helps the hair grip the string, producing a strong sound.*

ALBERT EINSTEIN (1879–1955) loved the violin. But because he was a spectacular scientist, people may have expected too much of him as a musician. When he played with other people, he sometimes got confused and played at the wrong times. Someone once asked him, "Professor, can't you count to three?" (A simple waltz is counted one, two, three; one, two, three.) A violin teacher at the University of Indiana played with Einstein and said he wasn't really so bad. Sometimes he would get so excited about the music, he would forget to play. Instead, he'd tell everyone how beautiful the music was.

Einstein was fascinated by the concepts of time and space. Does the speed of time ever change? Can space change at all?

His work did have many practical implications, however. Einstein developed the concepts behind early "electric eyes" that could be used to operate elevator doors or alarm systems. Some of his discoveries are the foundation of nuclear energy. They are written as his most famous equation, $E = MC^2$.

What You'll Need

tree branch, about 2 feet (0.6 m) long and slightly bent
spool of thread
rosin

What to Do

1 Tightly tie the thread to one end of the branch.

2 Bring the thread to the other end, pull it taut, and wrap it once around the end of the branch. Bring the thread to the starting end, pull it taut, and wrap it around again. Repeat these steps until you have about ten lengths of thread between the ends. Then cut the thread and tie it to the branch.

3 Rub some rosin on the "hairs" of your bow.

4 To play, hold the bow in your right hand and draw it back and forth on a string, making the nicest sound you can.

Bass

A string bass is not too different from a violin. It has all the same parts, only they're much bigger. The bass is 6 feet (1.8 m) high and can be played while standing or sitting on a tall stool. It can be plucked to make a ringing sound. (Bass means a low-pitched sound.) Jazz bands use this effect very often. It can also be played with a bow. Its deep, low sound makes it better at emphasizing rhythm than playing melodies.

The bass guitar, which is amplified, serves the same basic purpose as the string bass. It can play simple melodies very low to emphasize rhythm in a jazz or rock band.

Java Jive Bass

Here's an easy way to make a hoppin' bass to keep a cool beat. Experiment with different lengths of string and sticks. A larger can will make your bass sound deeper.

What You'll Need

2-pound (0.9-kg) coffee can

hammer

nail

5-foot (1.5-m) piece of heavy string

small stick, such as a craft stick

utility knife (to be used only by an adult)

long stick, such as a yardstick (meterstick)

adult helper

What to Do

1 Ask an adult to make a small hole in the center of the bottom of the coffee can by pounding the nail through it.

2 Tie one end of the string around the middle of the small stick, making many knots so that it is sure to hold.

3 Thread the free end of the string through the hole in the can so that the small stick is on the inside of the can.

4 Ask an adult to use the utility knife to make a small hole in one end of the long stick and a wedge-shaped notch in the other end of the stick, as shown.

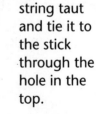

STEP 4

5 Set the long stick on the bottom of the can so that the notch is over the rim. Pull the string taut and tie it to the stick through the hole in the top.

6 Play your bass by plucking the string while holding the can down with one foot. Make different sounds by changing the string's tension. To do this, tilt the stick closer to or farther from the hole in the bottom of the can.

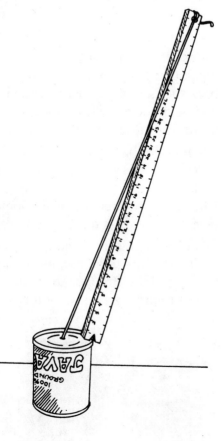

STEP 5

Harp

Harps play such beautiful music that people picture angels playing them, floating happily on their clouds. The harp is a very old instrument, dating back thousands of years to ancient Egypt. Some early versions were smaller and held horizontally on the player's lap instead of standing vertically in a frame like the larger modern harp.

The modern harp has 47 strings, which are color coded so that the player knows which is which. The strings are made of nylon and stay in tune better than early ones made from animal fibers. Before each concert, the harp must be carefully tuned. Sometimes the player uses an electronic device that checks the tuning of each string.

While the harpist is playing, the strings can be adjusted by foot pedals at the base of the frame. These change the tension in the strings. Stretching or relaxing the string changes the sound. (A tighter stretch causes a higher sound.) Harps can be beautifully decorated with carvings or inlaid wood.

Piano

Some people don't think of the piano as a stringed instrument because the strings don't show, but if you look inside a **grand piano**, it looks like a harp turned on its side and set in a big wooden case. A grand piano is a large piano in which the strings lie horizontally in a frame. In an **upright piano,** the strings are arranged vertically. Inside both types is a long row of felt-tipped hammers which strike the strings when the player presses the keys. (Because of this, some musicians consider the piano a percussion instrument.) Instruments that have this type of construction are called **keyboards.**

In the seventeenth century, the harpsichord was the most common keyboard instrument. It looks like a small, graceful piano. The biggest difference is that the piano mechanism strikes the strings, but the harpsichord mechanism plucks them.

The piano's strings are made of steel, and the lowest ones are covered with copper wire. The hammers for the low notes strike one or two heavy strings, but those for the high notes hit three thin strings. Strings that are hit at the same time have to be tuned to the same pitch, so tuning a piano can take a long time.

Three foot pedals on the piano are used to subtly change the sound. One foot pedal is used to create a ringing sound, and another one creates a soft, muffled sound. The third pedal allows selected strings to ring while the rest are dampened. This way, the pianist can change the sound to fit the music.

The modern piano is a much more powerful instrument than its nineteenth-century ancestors. It uses a heavy iron frame instead of one made of wood. This allows higher tension in the strings, making a louder and richer sound. Its keys are made of plastic rather than expensive ivory, because of laws designed to protect endangered animals.

Electronic keyboards are used today in different settings. A small church may use one to accompany the choir, and a band may use one because the keyboard is light and portable. The keyboard is connected to external speakers and an amplifier rather than strings, and can produce many different tone qualities.

Scientist's Corner — Inside a Piano

What's inside a piano?

What You'll Need

piano
large, soft eraser
sharpened pencil

What to Do

1. Ask permission to open the piano lid.

2. Look inside. You'll see lots of strings and hammers.

3. Stick the eraser on the point of the pencil.

4. Tap the strings on the far left and right with the eraser.

5. Press down the pedal on the far right. What happens inside the piano? Try shouting into the piano with the pedal down. What do you hear?

6. Notice the thin strings on the right. See how much thicker the strings on the left are.

What You Discovered

The thick strings on the far left sound very low when you tap them. The thin strings on the right sound very high. The pedal on the right moves a row of dampers (small felt-covered blocks that stop the vibrations of the strings) up and down. When the dampers are up, the strings keep vibrating after you press the keys. When they're down, the strings are muffled quickly. Shouting into the piano with the dampers up makes the strings **resonate** (vibrate together) with your voice. The vibrations of your voice start the strings vibrating.

The strings on the right are thin wires, with groups of three wires for each piano key. It's hard to keep these in tune, but three wires are needed to make a loud sound. The thick strings on the left sound very low and can easily make a loud sound.

ALEXANDER GRAHAM BELL (1847–1922) was so talented that his early piano teacher thought he should be a professional pianist. As a child, he'd stay up at night thinking about music. His mother thought he had "musical fever."

While just a youngster in Scotland, Bell and his brother tried to build a model human head to imitate speech. It had parts representing the organs necessary for speech, like soft lips, a mechanical tongue, and a windpipe. It made some sort of sound well enough for the neighbor to come running, asking why the baby was crying. Later, Bell experimented with his own mouth. He wanted to figure out which sounds were made when his tongue and lips were in certain positions. He even tried teaching his dog how to pronounce sounds.

Bell was interested in teaching the deaf to speak. He met Helen Keller (1880–1968), who couldn't see or hear, when she was only six years old. He also taught at a school for deaf children in Boston.

Bell's interest in speech led to his most famous invention. He had an idea for a telegraph system that could send more than one message at a time. In 1876, he invented a special kind of telegraph that could reproduce sounds rather than just make the clicks of Morse code. This was called the telephone, and it revolutionized the world.

Scientist's Corner — String Phone

How can we hear sound traveling along a string?

What You'll Need

15 feet (4.5 m) of thread

needle

2 paper clips

2 wax-coated paper cups

helper

adult helper

(*NOTE: Please ask for help using the needle.*)

What to Do

1 Thread the needle and tie a paper clip to one end of the thread.

2 With adult help, push the needle through the bottom of a cup from the inside.

3 Pull the thread till it is stopped by the paper clip.

4 Push the needle through the bottom of the second cup from the outside.

5 Remove the needle and tie a paper clip to the end of the thread.

6 To use, put one cup to your ear. Have a helper take the other cup and walk away from you, pulling the thread tight. Then have your helper talk into her cup.

What You Discovered
When your helper speaks into her cup, you clearly hear her in your cup.

Why?
The taut thread carries the sound waves of your helper's voice. The bottom of her cup acts like a drumhead. As it vibrates, it sends vibrations along the thread to the bottom of your cup. This vibrates the air inside, and the vibrations reach your ear. This demonstration depends on vibrations in the thread. Bell's telephone used electrical signals carried by wires. This makes the telephone very different from your string phone.

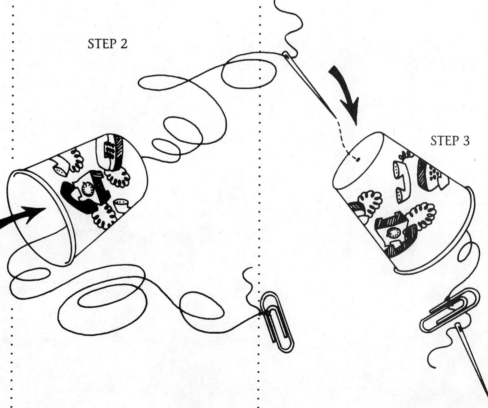

STEP 2

STEP 3

3

Wind Instruments

In wind instruments like the flute and trumpet, vibrating air takes the place of vibrating strings. Strings travel from side to side when they vibrate. Inside a flute or clarinet, the air doesn't travel from side to side. It moves back and forth instead, like compression waves in a Slinky. Remember how you had to jerk the Slinky in the experiment in chapter 1 to get the waves started. Blowing across a flute's blow hole sets up Slinky-like waves in the tube. In the clarinet, a vibrating **reed** (a thin piece of wood set in the mouthpiece) gets the waves started. Different pitches are played by pressing keys that open or close holes in the tube. This makes the air column inside the tube longer or shorter. Like strings, longer air columns produce lower pitches.

Length and Pitch

Does the length of a wind instrument affect how it sounds?

What You'll Need

scissors

drinking straw

What to Do

1 Cut a triangular point in one end of the straw.

STEP 1

2 Lightly pinch the pointed end of the straw between your lips. Blow into the straw to make a buzzing sound. You have to blow pretty hard to get a sound.

3 While blowing, cut off short pieces of straw at the other end. Listen to what happens.

What You Discovered

The sound gets higher as you cut pieces off the straw.

Why?

Just as with vibrating strings, a shorter straw produces a higher sound. The vibrations travel a shorter distance. The short column of air gives the sound a higher frequency and pitch.

Soda-Bottle Wind Music

♪ Here's a very simple wind instrument you can make. Remember, a longer column of air sounds lower. That's why a flute sounds lower than its little cousin the piccolo.

What You'll Need

3 soda bottles

water

What to Do

1 Fill the soda bottles with different levels of water.

2 Blow across the mouth of each bottle to make a foghorn sound. This may take some practice.

3 Notice how the sound is highest in the bottle with the most water.

STEP 2

Reed Instruments

Reeds are a lot of work. Even if reeds are bought ready-made by machine, professional players still have to adjust them. The reed's shape greatly influences the sound quality, so players shave the reed with a special knife to shape it properly. Players also keep the reed in their mouth so the reed stays wet. If the reed dries out, it gets too stiff and won't vibrate properly. A bad reed can really ruin a player's day.

Oboe

Remember the story of Peter and the Wolf? A narrator tells the story, and the characters are represented by different instruments of the orchestra. The duck (who gets swallowed by the wolf) is played by the oboe. Musicians joke about the oboe's sounding like a duck, and oboe players don't like it when their playing is compared to quacking.

The oboe uses a special kind of reed. A narrow piece of bamboo is folded and tied to a short metal pipe. This is pushed into the body of the oboe. The bamboo is cut at the fold, forming a double reed. The oboe makes a special sound very different from a clarinet or saxophone.

The oboe is very easy to hear, even when played softly. All the instruments in the orchestra are tuned by matching the oboe. The oboe player sometimes uses an electronic machine to check the accuracy of the pitch. Dials on the machine spin like mad if the pitch is incorrect.

Snake Charmer's Oboe

♫♫ *This oboe makes a haunting sound that will charm your listeners.*

What You'll Need

3-by-10-inch (7.5-by-25-cm) piece of lightweight poster board

12-inch (30-cm) taper (candle)

masking tape

scissors

ruler

drinking straw

walnut-size piece of modeling clay

What to Do

1 Wrap the poster board lengthwise around the candle. Tighten the poster board by twisting it around the candle so that the poster board tapers like the candle.

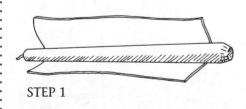

STEP 1

2 Tape the poster board at its seams. Slide the candle out of the tube.

3 Cut a 3-inch (7.5-cm) piece from the straw. Flatten one end and cut it to a point.

STEP 3

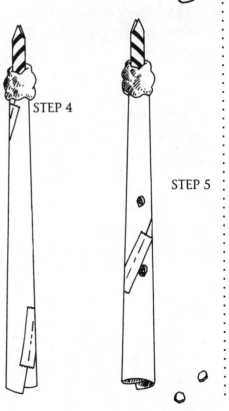

STEP 4

STEP 5

4 Insert the uncut end of the straw 1 inch (2.5 cm) into the narrow end of the poster board tube. Cover the opening at this end with the clay. Smooth the clay around the opening until it is totally covered.

5 Snip two small holes in the tube 4 inches (10 cm) and 6 inches (15 cm) from the straw, as shown.

6 To play, put the straw in your mouth and press your lips together. Blow to get a buzzing sound. Cover different holes with your fingers to play a tune.

Saxophone

• • • • •

The saxophone is the king of jazz instruments. Generally made of brass, some might have a bell made of silver, which makes a richer tone. They come in several sizes. The largest is the baritone, and the smallest is the soprano. Large ones have a deep, mellow tone. The smaller ones can play higher, yet still have a sweet tone.

The saxophone was invented in the mid-1800s by Adolphe Sax (1814–1894) of Belgium. He wanted to improve some existing instruments, including the clarinet. He succeeded, making the saxophone easy to play. But Sax failed to make much money from his invention, even though we see saxophones in almost every band and music store.

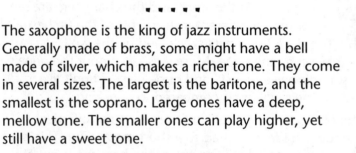

Clarinet

· · · · ·

The clarinet appeared in France and Germany in the seventeenth century. The sound is made by a vibrating reed set into the top of the mouthpiece. Keys open and close holes in the tube to change the pitch played. It's a beautiful instrument often made of ebony, a black wood from Africa. A great jazz musician named Benny Goodman (1909–1986) pioneered the clarinet as a solo instrument in the 1950s and '60s.

Clarinets come in different sizes, which are used for different effects. The small E-flat clarinet can sound raucous and shrill. The large bass clarinet sounds grumpy and clumsy. The clarinet most often used, the B-flat model, sounds silky and smooth. It portrays the cat in *Peter and the Wolf*.

WILLIAM N. LIPSCOMB In the 1960s, a young violin student was practicing in a deserted lecture hall at Harvard University. While he was working, an old man walked in through a tall window, which was level with the street outside. (There was a door right by it, but the window must have been more convenient.) The violinist kept practicing as the man walked down the aisle, stopping close by. Then, he took a black notebook out of his coat and asked the student his name and how he could be reached. The violinist had no idea who the man was, and wasn't sure he wanted to give out his name and address.

It turned out that the old man was a Harvard chemistry professor, William N. Lipscomb (1919–   ), who liked to play music with other talented musicians. He was himself a fine clarinetist. The violinist went to the professor's house, and after a nice dinner, they played music together.

In 1976, Lipscomb won the Nobel prize for chemistry. He explained a process not well understood about the way atoms can share electrons. How about the violin student? Years later, he wrote the book you're reading now.

Instruments without Reeds

· · · · ·

Flute

· · · · ·

Flutes date back thousands of years and are found around the world. The first flutes were made of bone or wood, and were played by blowing through one end. A later variation used a blow hole drilled in the side near one end. This new instrument was the ancestor of our modern flute.

Today's flute is made of metal. A good model is made of silver, but a really expensive one is made of gold or platinum. Some players think gold gives a more mellow tone than silver. Different pitches are played by using keys to open or close holes in the tube. This changes the length of the air column inside. High sounds require very good breath control. Flute students have lots of trouble playing high pitches.

The flute has a wonderful tone. Sometimes it's used in a playful imitation of birds. It can make a murmuring sound like water flowing in a stream. Flutes can even imitate shrill laughter or shrieking. A famous flute piece is named for a **faun**, a mythological creature having the upper body of a human and the lower body of an animal. In the flute piece he's relaxing during an enchanted, dreamy afternoon.

 *Build a clay flute that you can play yourself.*

What You'll Need

oven-bakeable polymer such as Sculpey or FIMO (available in a crafts supply store)

waxed paper

rolling pin

butter knife

ruler

cap of fine-line marking pen without clip

paintbrush

several colors of acrylic paints

adult helper

NOTE: This project requires an oven and adult supervision.

What to Do

1 Place the Sculpey on a sheet of waxed paper and roll it out into a thin rectangle.

2 Using the butter knife, cut the Sculpey to 3 inches (7.5 cm) wide and 14 inches (35 cm) long.

STEPS 3 AND 4

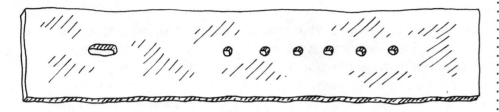

3 Use the cap of the marking pen to punch six holes along the midline of the rectangle. Make the first hole 6 inches (15 cm) from the left end, and make the others 1 inch (2.5 cm) apart, as shown.

4 On the midline, make one ¾-inch (2-cm)-long hole 2 inches (5 cm) from the left end.

5 Roll a small piece of Sculpey into a ball about 1 inch (2.5 cm) in diameter, then flatten it slightly to make a disc.

6 Place the disc at the end of the mouthpiece (the left end of the rectangle).

7 Gently roll the rectangle around the disc until the edges touch. It will now look like a hollow tube closed by the disc at the left end. Rub your finger along the seam to close it.

8 Ask an adult to follow the directions on the Sculpey package to bake your flute.

9 After the flute cools, decorate it by painting it with acrylics.

10 To play the flute, hold it with the mouthpiece end to your left, your left-hand palm facing you, and the right-hand palm facing away from you. Use your right-hand fingers to cover the finger holes near the right end of the flute and the left-hand fingers to cover the holes near the mouthpiece. You won't use your pinkies. Blow over the mouthpiece the way you would a soda bottle. Experiment to get the best sound, and cover different holes to play a tune.

TO PLAY

STEPS 6 AND 7

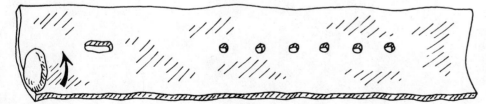

Trumpet

Trumpets are heard in marching bands, jazz groups, and large symphonic orchestras. Early versions have been found around the world. Very old trumpets were made of wood, metal, or horn. Early models didn't have valves like today's trumpets.

Valves, which adjust the amount of air vibrating inside the tube, were added in the early 1800s. Valves make it easier to play higher and lower sounds.

Trumpets come in a variety of sizes. A small one, called the piccolo trumpet, was used in the 17th century to play very high, ornamental music. Trumpets are very versatile. They can play loud music, designed to catch your attention, or quieter music that sounds dreamy. The trumpet's sound can be adjusted with metal mutes, which are pushed into the bell (the flared end of a wind instrument). These muffle the sound. One special mute makes a funny sound that's like laughter: wa-wa-wa!

You play the trumpet by blowing and buzzing your lips. It takes practice to control all the muscles around your mouth.

Keeping Your Chops Up

If a trumpeter hasn't been practicing, his mouth muscles get out of shape. When this happens, people say the trumpeter has "lost his chops."

French Horn

· · · · ·

Horns were originally made of hollowed-out animal tusks and horns. They were used to send signals during hunting trips and military events. They didn't have finger holes, so they could play only a few different sounds. Players adjusted their lips and breathing to change the sounds. These early horns were often decorated with carvings or inlaid metal.

Metal horns appeared in France around 1650. They had a circular shape, and could play music as well as hunting signals. Metal tubes were added, which adjusted the horn's length. They allowed different sounds to be played. These tubes, and later valves, allowed the horn to play a melody like other instruments.

Players put the right hand inside the large bell to soften and adjust the sound. Even in a large concert hall, a French horn will sound very rich and strong. In orchestras, horns are often used in a group of four. That way they can play rich-sounding chords as well as melodies written specially for them. French horns are used in *Peter and the Wolf* to portray the hungry wolf.

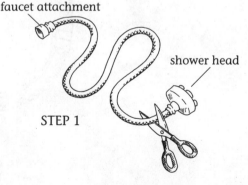

2 Slide the funnel over the end of the hose opposite the faucet attachment.

3 Loop the hose into a circle, pulling the faucet attachment and funnel so that they point up.

4 Tape the circle together about 6 inches (15 cm) from the faucet attachment. Tape again, 6 inches (15 cm) from the funnel.

5 Snip a small hole in the inner section of hose just above the tape nearest the faucet attachment.

6 To play, hold the horn by the two taped areas. Hold the tape under the funnel with your left hand, and the tape under the faucet attachment with your right hand. Cover the finger hole with your index finger, then blow into the faucet attachment, letting your lips vibrate. Lift your finger off the hole for a different sound.

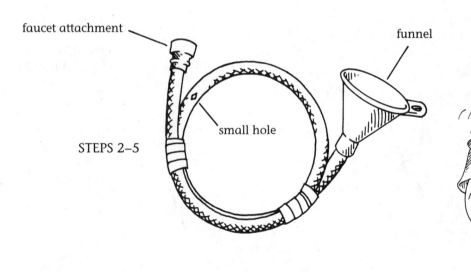

faucet attachment

funnel

small hole

STEPS 2–5

Tuba

· · · · ·

There are many versions of the tuba, but they're all big. They sound either very low or just plain low. Tubas were developed in Germany in the early 1800s and were used in different versions for brass marching bands. John Philip Sousa (1854–1932), who wrote marches you might hear on the Fourth of July, made his own type of tuba. The sousaphone fits over the player's shoulders. Other models are held on the player's lap. The player blows into a big metal mouthpiece and presses valves. These open and shut different coils of brass tubing, changing the length of the vibrating air column.

The tuba usually plays the bass tones in a brass group. This is not the most interesting music, and it can be compared to low grunts and groans. A charming musical story, *Tubby the Tuba*, portrays the misery of a little tuba who would love to play a nice melody for a change. He finally finds a lively melody to play and becomes the happiest tuba in history.

Pipe Organ

· · · · ·

The pipe organ is a majestic instrument that can cover the wall of a huge church. Hundreds or even thousands of pipes of different sizes produce different pitches and tone qualities when air is passed through them. The pipes are arranged in graceful rows, forming a beautiful design. The organist sits in front of a complicated console consisting of two or three separate keyboards. The player also uses her feet to press a row of pedals which play the deep bass tones. Today, electronic organs may take the place of the huge pipe organ. Tones are produced electronically (there aren't any pipes) and played through a speaker system.

Flip-Floppin' Organ Pipes

🎵🎵🎵 *Here's a wind instrument that you don't have to blow into. Just let a recycled pair of last summer's flip-flops do all the work. A quick trip down the plumbing aisle of a hardware store will provide the other materials you'll need.*

What You'll Need

small hand saw (to be used only by an adult)

ruler

10-foot (3-m) PVC pipe, 1½ inches (3.75 cm) in diameter

4 plastic 1½-inch (3.75-cm) elbow-joint fittings for PVC pipe

corrugated cardboard box, at least 18 inches (45 cm) long at the top

marking pen

scissors

masking tape

pair of flip-flops (rubber thong sandals)

adult helper

What to Do

1 Have an adult use the hand-saw to cut the PVC pipe in the following four lengths: 36¼ inches (90.6 cm), 32 inches (80 cm), 28¾ inches (71.9 cm), 22¾ inches (56.9 cm).

2 Slide a plastic elbow joint onto one end of each length of pipe.

STEP 2

3 Open the top and bottom flaps of the box. Draw four squares measuring 1¾ inches (4.4 cm) along the edge of one flap, spacing them evenly as shown. Cut out these squares.

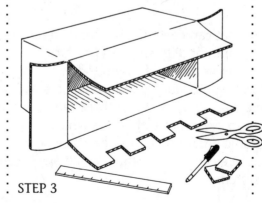

STEP 3

4 Turn the box over. Cut four identical squares on the opposite flap. Cut out these squares.

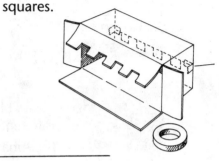

5 Tape all flaps closed.

6 Slide each pipe into the box through one hole then out of the box through the opposite hole. The longest length should be at the left. Put the pipes in order from the longest to the shortest. The elbow joints should be faceup.

7 Number each pipe with number 1 being the longest and number 4 the shortest.

8 To play, slap the opening of each elbow joint with a flip-flop to make a sound. Your pipes are tuned to play "Mary Had a Little Lamb." Hit each pipe as its number appears below.

3-2-1-2-3-3-3	Mary had a little lamb,
2-2-2	Little lamb,
3-4-4	Little lamb,
3-2-1-2-3-3-3	Mary had a little lamb
3-2-2-3-2-1	Whose fleece was white as snow.

As a young man, ALBERT SCHWEITZER (1875–1965) was a religion student who loved to play the pipe organ. Schweitzer was only eight when he started to play the organ. As an adult, he taught philosophy and religion. He still continued performing on the organ and writing about music. His teaching and musical life made Schweitzer very respected and successful.

When he was 30, Schweitzer decided he wanted to contribute more to the world. He went to medical school so that he could be a doctor in Africa helping people with tropical diseases. He made it to Africa, where he enjoyed his work at the hospital. His patients arrived in canoes from up and down the river. Sometimes he got paid with eggs and bananas. Unfortunately, his work was disrupted when he was taken as a prisoner during the First World War. He was sent to a prison camp in France. There, he treated the prisoners' illnesses and met people from all over the world.

After the war, Schweitzer traveled back to Africa many times, earning money for his hospital by giving concerts and lectures. For his medical work and lectures about the evils of war, he was awarded the Nobel Peace prize in 1953. He played concerts, made recordings, and gave lectures all through his long life.

STEP 6

4
Percussion Instruments

The percussion instruments include the xylophone, the drum, the gong, the triangle … and just about anything else you can bang on.

The percussion family includes melody instruments like the xylophone, and rhythm instruments like the bass drum. Rhythm instruments make a sound with no definite pitch. They mark and emphasize the music's **rhythm** (the timing of music, showing how it changes and moves).

Some drums are tuned by adjusting the tension of the membrane (a thin, flexible sheet of animal skin or plastic). The membrane is commonly referred to as the drumhead. When played, the instruments are struck by a mallet or stick. Percussion instruments don't have to sound loud, though. A triangle or cymbal can be tapped delicately, giving a quiet, faraway sound.

Many materials are used to build percussion instruments. Drums have plastic or animal hide membranes stretched tightly across a hollow plastic, wooden, or metal cylinder. Instruments like the xylophone and marimba have tuned wood or metal plates. Gongs and cymbals are made of brass. Castanets, used to make a clicking sound, are made of hardwood. The percussion instruments follow the basic rules about length of instrument and pitch played. A longer xylophone plate gives a lower pitch than a shorter one. A tighter membrane on a drum gives a higher pitch. A thicker membrane gives a lower pitch.

Drums
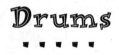

Drums can be shaped in many ways. The bass drum is a big cylinder with a membrane on both sides. Other drums are shaped like an ice-cream cone or hourglass, and can have one or two membranes. One type of "hour-glass" drum has straps connected to the drumhead which can be tightened, changing the drum's sound.

Some drums seem to have no shape at all. Some Native American tribes use hollowed sections of a tree trunk to make their drums. An animal skin is cut to fit the shape of the tree trunk. These drums have some very unusual shapes.

The timpani, or kettledrums, are huge metal "kettles" with a plastic membrane stretched across the open top. The player can use a foot pedal to adjust the tension while playing.

Bongos are two small drums joined together. They're held on the player's lap or between the knees, and slapped with both hands. Bongos are used in all kinds of music, including jazz and folk music, especially from the Caribbean islands.

Band on the Run

In a big orchestra, percussion players have to run back and forth between the different instruments, sometimes arriving just in time to whack one. This is so entertaining that the audience can forget to pay attention to the music.

Drums can have vibrating parts in addition to the membrane stretched over them. Snare drums have metal springs stretched underneath the drumheads. They cause a loud rattle when the drum is played. The tambourine is a handheld drum. The metal discs attached to the frame cause another type of rattling, or splashing, sound.

Scientist's Corner

Stretched Soda Bottles

Why are drumheads stretched?

What You'll Need

unopened plastic bottle of soda
empty bottle of the same type as the unopened one, with cap
water
butter knife

What to Do

1 Set the bottles next to each other, then fill the empty bottle with water to the same level as the unopened bottle. Replace the cap.

2 Tap the side of the unopened bottle with the butter knife. Notice the sound.

3 Tap the water-filled bottle and notice the sound.

What You Discovered

Tapping the unopened bottle made a clear, ringing sound.

Why?

Sodas are made with carbonated water. A gas is dissolved into water and kept in the bottle under pressure. When you open the bottle, pressurized gas escapes in bubbles. The unopened bottle's sides are tightly stretched by the gas pressure inside the water. The other bottle's sides are not stretched. A stretched membrane gives a drum its clear sound.

Talking Drums

In many early civilizations, drums were used for communication. The African talking drum is made from a log that is partially hollowed out. Slits are cut into the top, and the log is struck with short sticks. The sound is loud enough to travel several miles (kilometers) through the forest. The talking drums send messages in code.

Do large objects sound lower than small ones when they're struck?

What You'll Need

tape

two 12-inch (30-cm) lengths of
    string

2 empty milk cartons, one 1 pint
    (500 ml) and one one-half
    gallon (1.9 liters)

pencil

What to Do

1 Tape a string to the top of
each carton, making a loop.
The cartons are the drums.

STEP 1

2 Hang the drums from your
outstretched arm.

3 Tap each drum with the pencil and notice the sound it
makes.

STEPS 2 AND 3

What You Discovered

The larger drum sounded lower
than the smaller one.

Why?

The larger drum has a larger drumhead (the side of the carton). Also,
the larger space inside the larger
drum makes the air vibrate slower.

Now Try This

Try tapping the drums with the
flaps closed, and then open. Closed
flaps trap the sound inside, so it
seems softer.

*Do bottles make different sounds
when you blow into them rather
than tap them?*

What You'll Need

3 glass soda bottles

water

butter knife

What to Do

1 Fill the 3 bottles to different
levels with water.

2 Blow across the mouth of
each bottle to make a foghorn
sound. Notice how the water level
affects the sound.

3 Tap the butter knife against
each bottle to produce a
ringing sound. Notice the effect
of the water level.

What You Discovered

When you blew across the mouth
of the bottle, more water made a
higher sound. When you struck

the bottle, more water made a lower sound.

Why?

Adding water shortens the air column. When you blow across the bottle, you are making the air vibrate. A shorter air column makes higher sounds. This is similar to what happens in wind instruments such as the flute. When you strike the bottle, you make the glass vibrate. More water slows the vibrations in the glass. Slower vibrations make a lower sound.

Trash Can Jam

🎵🎵 *Drumheads used to be made from animal skins. These would shrink as they dried out, making a higher sound. The drumhead for this project is made from canvas. It shrinks when water is sprayed on it—just the opposite of an animal skin.*

What You'll Need

tape measure
round, small, kitchen trash can or

plastic bucket
canvas remnant (available in a fabric store)
duct tape
spray bottle filled with water
2 pencils, spoons, or sticks

What to Do

1 Measure the diameter (the distance across the center of a circle) of the opening in the trash can. Cut a square of canvas 4 inches (10 cm) larger than the diameter.

2 Lay the canvas across the top of the can so that the edges hang evenly over the rim.

STEPS 2 AND 3

3 Tape one corner of the canvas firmly to the side of the can.

4 Tape the opposite corner to the opposite side, pulling the canvas taut as you tape it down. Repeat for the other two corners.

5 Pull taut any loose edges of canvas and tape them so the drumhead is tight.

STEP 6

6 Spray the canvas with water to tighten it.

7 To play, tap the drumhead with the pencils or slap it with your hands for a bongo effect.

Popcorn Shaker

 Rattles come in all shapes and sizes. Musicians from long ago used whatever nature provided. The following version is made with popcorn. After you've tried this project, experiment by using other natural materials. Seedpods can turn into rattles when they dry. Or take two halves of a walnut shell and make castanets. The possibilities are endless.

What You'll Need

round balloon

ruler

string

papier-mâché paste (see recipe)

newspaper

paintbrush

white and several other colors of paint

scissors

¼ cup (63 ml) popcorn (unpopped)

masking tape

What to Do

1 Inflate the balloon to the size of a football. Tie a knot in the neck of the balloon.

2 Tie a 10-inch (25-cm) length of string to the neck.

3 Make papier-mâché paste from the recipe shown.

4 Tear the newspaper into 1-inch (2.5-cm) strips.

5 Dip one strip at a time into the paste and apply the strip to the balloon. The newspaper and paste make papier-mâché.

6 Add papier-mâché until the entire balloon, except for the neck area, is covered.

STEP 5

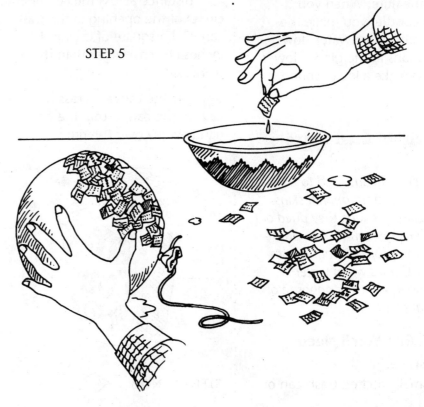

Recipe for Papier-Mâché Paste

What You'll Need

small bowl
½ cup (125 ml) flour
1 tablespoon (15 ml) salt
1 cup (250 ml) water

What to Do

1 Use the bowl to mix the flour and salt.

2 Add water to the flour-and-salt mixture and mix with your hands. The paste should be the consistency of a thin milkshake.

7 Hang the balloon by its string to dry.

8 Add another layer of papier-mâché over the first. Hang the balloon to dry again.

9 Paint a base coat of white over the entire surface. Add colorful splashes to decorate. Hang the balloon to dry.

10 Pop the balloon by cutting off the knot.

11 Pour popcorn into the balloon through the neck opening and tape the hole closed.

12 To play, hold the shaker in both hands and shake it.

STEP 11

Tambourine

 The tambourine is a handheld drum about 12 inches (30 cm) in diameter. Slapping the membrane produces the sound of a drum. Shaking the frame makes the metal discs produce a great "splashing" sound.

What You'll Need

foil pie pan
paintbrush
several colors of acrylic paint
scissors
yarn
paper clips
transparent tape
scarf

What to Do

1. Decorate the outside of the pie pan with acrylic paint.

2. Cut a 20-inch (50 cm) piece of yarn. Tape one end of the yarn to the outside of the pan below the rim.

3. String 3 paper clips onto the yarn, then tape the yarn past these clips to the pan. Thread another 3 clips and tape the yarn again. Repeat every 2 inches (5 cm), adding clips all around the outside of the pan.

4. Tape one corner of the scarf to the edge of the pan.

5. To play, tap or shake the tambourine in time to your favorite music.

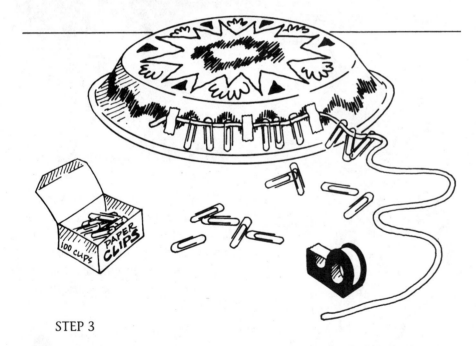

STEP 3

Feynman's Bongos

What You'll Need

scissors
2 round oatmeal cartons with plastic-ringed lids
plastic bag
masking tape

What to Do

1. Cut the inside circle out of each lid, leaving just the plastic ring.

RICHARD FEYNMAN (1918–1988) was a scientist who loved bongo drums and Brazilian music. Feynman was sometimes considered the crazy, wild man of science. He thought life was so much fun, he might as well try everything. Some of his scientific ideas seemed crazy to everybody else, but sometimes everyone else was wrong.

Feynman taught himself to play bongo and conga drums. He would play for dance performances, for friends at a party, or just for himself. Working at Los Alamos in the New Mexico desert, he was even heard playing the bongos while prancing around a tree late at night.

When he was in his 20s, he traveled to a laboratory in Chicago, where several scientists were stumped by a tough mathematical problem. One of them had been trying for a month to solve it. Feynman taught him how on the spot.

Just before his 30th birthday, Feynman presented his new ideas to a distinguished group of scientists. They thought he was poorly prepared and his presentation had basic flaws. Years later, when other scientists finally figured out what he meant, he won the Nobel prize.

2 Cut circles out of the bottoms of the containers.

3 Cut two 10-inch (25-cm)-square pieces out of the plastic bag.

4 Place one piece of plastic over the top of one container, then fit the plastic ring back over the container. Pull the plastic tight by tugging on its edges.

5 Repeat step 4 for the second container.

6 Tape the two drums together.

STEP 6

7 To play, use your hands to tap the drums on the drumheads and sides to your favorite music.

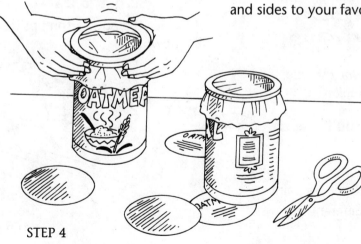

STEP 4

The Xylophone
. . . . .

The xylophone is one percussion instrument that's great for playing melodies. Sometimes players "show off" by playing exciting music written for other instruments.

The xylophone has a long row of tuned bars made of wood or metal. The bars are arranged like a piano keyboard, with the lowest sounds on the left and the highest on the right. Mallets (light hammers with small ball-shaped heads) are used to strike the bars. Some mallets are hard and make a brittle sound. Others are padded and make a soft, ringing sound. Metal tubes can be placed under the bars to reinforce the sound.

Handyman's Xylophone

♪ *This xylophone uses materials found in a toolbox.*

What You'll Need

egg carton
paintbrush
many colors of tempera paint
5 wrenches of different sizes
2 butter knives

What to Do

1 Place the egg carton upside down.

2 Decorate the egg carton with splashes of paint.

3 Lay each wrench across the bottom of the carton, between the partitions. Line the wrenches up according to size from longest to shortest.

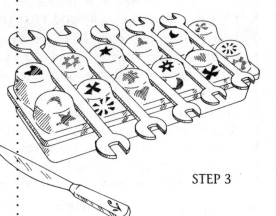

STEP 3

4 To play, strike the wrenches with the butter knives to produce a ringing sound.

STEP 1

Chimes

. . . . .

Chimes belong to a group of percussion instruments that are made of metal and sound like a bell when struck. Some instruments, such as chimes and bell sets, have a definite pitch. Others, such as the gong or cymbal, have no definite pitch. A gong or cymbal can really grab the audience's attention. A chime or triangle can imitate a doorbell or clock. These instruments can add a colorful quality to the overall effect of the music.

Mother Nature's Chimes

🎵 🎵 *Hang this instrument outdoors and let Mother Nature play it.*

What You'll Need

paintbrush

several colors of acrylic paint

3 clay flowerpots, from 2 ½ up to 4 inches (6.25 to 10 cm) tall

scissors

ruler

string

6 small screw nuts

white glue

3 pinecones

15-inch (37.5-cm) -long tree branch

What to Do

1 Paint all 3 pots and let the paint dry. The pots will hang upside down, so keep this in mind when making your designs.

2 Cut the string into three 20-inch (50-cm) lengths. Tie a large knot in one end of each string.

3 Thread a nut onto one string and tie it 2 inches (5 cm) from the knotted end. This is the bell's clapper (a metal object hung inside a bell to hit against the sides of the bell as it is rung).

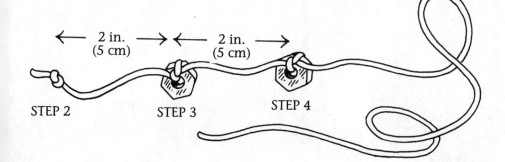

← 2 in. (5 cm) → ← 2 in. (5 cm) →

STEP 2   STEP 3   STEP 4

4 Thread a second nut onto the string and tie it 4 inches (10 cm) from the knotted end.

5 Insert the free end of the string through the hole in the pot so that the clapper is inside.

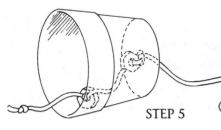

STEP 5

6 Glue the knotted end of the string to the top of a pinecone. You have made a bell.

7 Repeat steps 3 to 6 to make the other 2 bells.

8 Tie the free ends of each string to the tree branch, letting the bells hang down 8 to 10 inches.

9 Cut a 20-inch (50-cm) length of string. Tie each end to the branch to form a handle.

10 Hang your chimes outdoors where they will catch the wind.

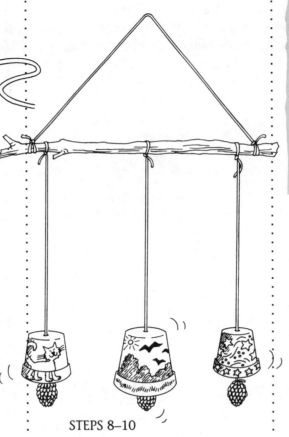

STEPS 8–10

Disappointing Redecoration

• • • •

Sometimes decorations can change sounds in surprising ways. The famous auditorium Carnegie Hall was redecorated recently. Changing the upholstery and painted surfaces changed the sound quality of the auditorium. Many musicians and listeners felt the sound quality suffered, even though the auditorium looked magnificent.

Gong

A gong is a huge metal dish hung in a frame. Striking it with a large, padded mallet produces a crashing sound. Because it's so heavy and made of metal, the gong creates a thunderous, ringing sound.

Mysterious Water Gong

♪ *This instrument makes a great eerie sound by using water to muffle the gong.*

What You'll Need

screw driver
large metal pot lid with
   screw-on handle
20-inch (50-cm) piece of string
sock
sharpened pencil
5-inch (12.5-cm)-square piece
   of fabric
masking tape
white glue
yarn
large pan of water

What to Do

1 Ask permission to unscrew and remove the handle of the pot lid.

2 Thread the string through the screw hole in the lid. Tie the ends of the string together.

3 Roll the sock into a ball and stick it onto the pencil.

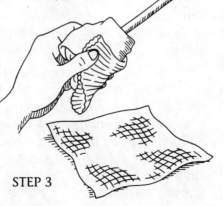

STEP 3

4 Cover the sock with the piece of fabric. Tape the edges of the fabric to the pencil. This is your mallet.

5 Glue the yarn over the tape to decorate the mallet and hide the tape.

STEP 6

6 To play, hold the pot lid by the string, and strike the edge of the lid with the mallet to make a loud, ringing sound. To muffle the sound, slowly dip the lid into the water while it is still ringing.

Imagination Game

♪ *This game is fun to play with a small group of friends. The trick is to let your imagination fly. The longer you play, the sillier it gets.*

What You'll Need

1 common household item for each player, such as a toothbrush, balloon (not inflated), rubber glove, plastic jar of popcorn, sheet of newspaper, or small paper bag

radio (optional)

5 or 6 players

NOTE: It's fun to have some lively music playing on the radio during the game.

What to Do

1 Without telling the players what the game is about, ask them to sit in a circle on the floor. Put the pile of items in the center and ask each player to choose one.

2 Tell the players that they must design a musical instrument from the item they are holding. They can do anything with the item to make a sound. Let everyone know that they can be as wacky as they'd like. Show them an example, such as the jar of popcorn. They can tap it, shake it, and vibrate their lips against it. They can open the jar and drop popcorn kernels onto its lid, and much more!

3 Go around the circle, letting everybody have a chance to demonstrate his invention. Cheer the players on as they perform.

When everyone has had a chance, play your instruments together.

4 To continue the fun, have everyone pass his item to the player on the left.

5 Repeat the process, using the item differently to make a different sound.

6 Play a few rounds until it gets ridiculous. You'll be amazed how creative everyone is.

LEONARDO DA VINCI (1452–1519) is famous for his fabulous paintings, such as the *Last Supper* and the *Mona Lisa*. He was also an impressive sculptor and a scientist.

As a scientist, Leonardo invented dozens of mechanical devices. Some were construction tools, like cranes and drills. One of his favorite inventions was a water pump designed to drain swamps. He was also interested in astronomy (the study of objects beyond the earth) and anatomy (the study of the structural makeup of living things). He became an expert in anatomy, drawing illustrations of the muscle system and internal organs.

Leonardo was a fine musician, both as a performer and a teacher. He sang while playing along on instruments he designed himself. Leonardo invented all sorts of instruments. One was made of silver and shaped like a horse's head. Another was a trumpet with keys instead of valves. Yet another amazing invention was a keyboard instrument meant to sound like a violin. He also designed mechanical drums that could play different rhythms while being rolled along on wheels. Leonardo was a truly creative musician.

5 Electronic Music

Beginnings Of Electronic Music

Technology has done more than improve our favorite old instruments. It's helped create a whole group of new ones, thanks to the discovery of electricity. The electronic piano and organ come from the same background as our new electronic music.

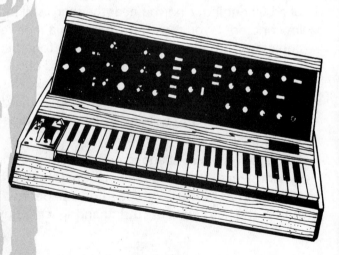

Composers (musicians who make up new musical pieces) turned to electronic devices to help them create new sounds. Many people thought our favorite instruments, like the violin and flute, sounded old-fashioned. Electronic instruments could create sounds never heard before, but the most popular electronic instruments usually imitate familiar instruments.

Ways to Make New Sounds
. . . . .

The search for new sounds began when musicians experimented by playing a record at the wrong speed. Played too fast, it might sound like a swarm of angry insects. Too slow, it might sound like low bellowing from Mars. Another trick was playing a record backward to produce really strange sounds.

Tape recorders were also used to create new sounds. Imagine the sound of a bell ringing. First you hear the sharp striking of the bell, and then the low ringing. If you record the bell with a tape recorder, you can cut the audiotape into pieces and piece it back together in a new way to make a new sound. You could remove the sound of the striker hitting the bell and just leave the ringing sound. You could take the striking sound and glue it to the sound of a whistling teakettle. Any sounds can be combined by cutting and **splicing** (joining together) the tape to achieve the desired effect. Combining sounds is easy.

Later, sounds were changed around using electronic instruments called **synthesizers**. A sound's pitch, loudness, and other qualities were adjusted according to instructions coded on a paper roll. Synthesizers saved composers the hard work of cutting and splicing tiny pieces of audiotape.

The Mysterious Theremin
. . . .

One early electronic instrument was invented in 1927 by a Russian scientist, Leon Theremin (1896–1993). His instrument, called the theremin, was so popular it's hard to believe that he himself was barely known. His mysterious personal story includes secret scientific laboratories and maybe even years in prison.

The theremin is a big box with a few antennae sticking out. It produces electronic vibrations which are influenced by the position of the player's arms. Waving the arms around the box produces haunting sounds. The theremin has been used in movies whenever a scary or ghostly sound is needed. It was even used in a song by the Beach Boys: "Good Vibrations."

Some types of electronic music use an interesting sound called **white noise** (an even blend of sound waves from the lowest frequency to the highest). It sounds like shhhh . . . , the hissing you hear between radio stations. Composers created the sounds they wanted, using white noise and electronic devices.

Composers use all sorts of different sounds experimentally. Recordings of live musicians might be blended with electronic imitations, making it difficult to tell which is which. Sounds of trains, machinery, clocks, and even airplane propellers have been used. Sounds might be slowed down or played backward.

 **Scientist's Corner**

Making White-Noise Music

How can you make your own electronic "music"?

What You'll Need
radio with bass and treble dials

What to Do

1 Set your radio between stations. You'll hear a *shhhh* sound.

2 Turn the bass dial up and down as you listen to the sound.

3 Turn the treble dial up and down while listening.

What You Discovered
You were able to alter the white noise using the bass and treble dials on your radio.

Why?
When you turn the treble dial up, the highest sounds are emphasized. When the bass dial is turned up, the lowest sounds are emphasized. This is similar to the way composers alter sounds electronically.

Your Own Electronic Studio

 Create your own sounds using a tape recorder. They can be part of your musical combo or enjoyed just by themselves!

What You'll Need
tape recorder
microphone (can be built into the recorder)
uncooked rice
inflated balloon
sheet of aluminum foil
large plastic trash can

What to Do
Try making your own sound effects and recording them on your tape recorder. Pour the rice over the balloon, crinkle the aluminum foil, and slap the trash can. There's no limit to the sounds you can create using different materials.

Electronic Music Today

You hear electronic music all the time on radio and TV. Popular bands often use modern synthesizers, which are much easier to use than the earlier ones. The old models could only play one sound at a time, and the tone quality was changed by rearranging numerous cables connecting the instrument's different parts. Now, the push of a button or switch accomplishes the same thing.

Today, electronic musical instruments can be connected together, or to personal computers, thanks to **MIDI** (musical instrument digital interface—a way of connecting electronic instruments to each other or to a computer). A musician can play on a keyboard while the computer prints out the music exactly as it's played. Imagine how much easier this is than handwriting each page. Changes can be made at the computer terminal, so correcting mistakes is no problem.

MIDI also permits electronic instruments to create amazing sound effects. A simple-looking keyboard might produce music that sounds like a whole orchestra. Beethoven would be amazed!

Printed Parts

Composers used to write down their own music by hand. Sometimes they got in trouble because they took too long. Rossini (1792–1868), one of Italy's favorite composers, was locked up in a tower overlooking a village square because he didn't get his parts written in time. He had to work, dropping written sheet music out a window, until he finished. Beethoven (1770–1827) had trouble getting his music written on time, too. One concert had to be performed without a rehearsal. Because the music was delivered late, the players read Beethoven's scribbling by candlelight.

6

Recording Music

Most of the music we hear now is recorded. But recorded sound has only been around since 1877, when Thomas Edison (1847–1931) invented the first phonograph (a device that uses a vibrating needle and a grooved cylinder or disc to reproduce sound).

Phonographs
. . . . .

Some early phonographs looked like a big cone sitting on a platform. The cone acted just like your ear, concentrating sound onto a small area. Inside the cone's small end was a device that worked like your eardrum by vibrating along with the sound waves in the air. This device pushed a sharp point against metal foil wrapped around a turning cylinder. The point etched grooves in the foil that matched sound waves in the air. When the recording was finished, the cylinder could be turned to play back the original sound.

Further developments in the phonograph used different materials and shapes in the search for the best record. Wax and hard plastic cylinders were tried, but discs worked best. By 1915, plastic discs called 78s were common. They turned 78 times per minute and could store about 4 minutes' worth of music. A needle made of metal, or even cactus, vibrated inside the disc's groove.

It was important to keep the record turning at a constant speed. Edison wanted to use an electric motor, but a spring-driven motor was the first practical choice. Electric motors weren't commonly used until the 1940s. Another problem was solved in the 1920s with the invention of microphones. Before then, performers had to huddle around a big cone connected to the recorder. They'd sing or play into it, hoping to be heard loudly enough compared to their neighbor. With microphones, performers could stand farther away and all their sounds would be recorded properly.

Long-playing records (LPs) came about in the late 1940s. These could store 25 minutes or more of music. The next development was stereo, about 10 years later. A stereo LP is a double recording in which each record groove actually holds two separate tracks (paths on which sound is recorded). Just as two ears improve your hearing, two tracks give a more realistic impression of the sound. Stereo, which uses two or more speakers, made it easier to tell where different sounds were coming from. A stereo recording of three people singing separates their voices clearly, so you could point to the position of each singer.

Seeing Sound

How can you see a sound?

What You'll Need
can opener

coffee can

plastic wrap

large rubber band

glue stick

silver-colored sequin

flashlight

several books

helper

What to Do

1 Remove both ends of the coffee can.

2 Tear off a piece of plastic wrap large enough to fit over one end of the can. Stretch the wrap over the end of the can, and secure it with the rubber band.

3 Glue the sequin onto the center of the plastic wrap.

STEPS 2 AND 3

4 In a dark room, set the can on its side so that the sequin faces the wall. Use books to keep it from rolling.

5 Have your helper shine the flashlight onto the sequin while you shout, sing, and talk into the open end of the coffee can. Try not to blow into the can. Just be loud.

What You Discovered

You saw the light reflected on the wall wiggle as you shouted into the coffee can.

Why?

The plastic wrap and sequin vibrate along with the sound waves from your voice. A phonograph needle behaves the same way. It vibrates according to the shape of the grooves in the record. These grooves correspond to the sound waves recorded by the microphone.

STEP 5

Tape Recorders

▪ ▪ ▪ ▪ ▪

Magnetic tape stores sound in a mysterious way. Microphones convert sound waves in the air to electrical signals. The signals and sound waves have the same basic shape. These signals are sent to the tape recorder. Motors in the tape recorder pull a thin strip of magnetic tape across electromagnets. Their magnetism changes according to the signals sent by the microphone, forming patterns that are stored on the tape. To hear the sounds played back, the tape is sent through the recorder again. This time, another electromagnet "reads," or reproduces, the patterns on the tape. These patterns are strengthened by an amplifier and sent on to speakers, from which the original sounds are heard.

Compact Discs

▪ ▪ ▪ ▪ ▪

Compact discs (CDs) use a whole new process to store sounds. Instead of magnetic tape or grooves on a record, CDs use numbers. This process is called digital recording. When it first appeared, some people thought it couldn't reproduce music properly. Others thought the new process would make recordings more realistic and reduce background noise.

There were problems with the old analog recording process used by phonographs and earlier tape recorders. Tapes and records produced by this process tend to be noisy and can't reproduce soft or loud sounds accurately. The grooves on a record get dirty or scratched, while magnetic patterns on an old tape can get blurred and garbled.

In the digital recording process, special recording machines are used to convert sounds into a string of numbers. CDs store numbers using the **binary number system**. In this system, any number can be represented by a string of 0s and 1s. The numbers are stored on the CD in a code of shiny and dark spots. The spots are too small for the human eye to see and are read by a laser light beam. The laser is reflected by the shiny spots on the CD, and not by the dark ones. The resulting sound is clearer and less distorted than with analog recording.

Modern tape recorders can use this technology also. Digitized sounds are stored on tape, giving a less noisy and more accurate sound.

Zeros and Ones

How does the binary number system work?

What You'll Need
pencil and paper

What to Do
Decode the two binary numbers (shown as rows of 0s and 1s) by adding the numbers above the 1s.

1 In the first example, there are 1s under the 8, 4, and 1 columns. Thus 8 + 4 + 1 = 13.

2 In the second example, there are 1s under the 4, 2, and 1 columns. Thus, 4 + 2 + 1 = 7.

Binary Code for "13"

16s	8s	4s	2s	1s
	1	1	0	1

$$8 + 4 + 1 = 13$$

Binary Code for "7"

16s	8s	4s	2s	1s
		1	1	1

$$4 + 2 + 1 = 7$$

What You Discovered
The number 13 is written 1101 in binary code. The number 7 is written 111.

Why?
Binary code uses two digits to represent numbers. These two digits, 1 and 0, can be thought of as yes and no, or on and off. The binary code system is shown in the column heads of the chart, starting with 1 on the right. Because only two digits are used, each number to the left is twice the number to the right.

Converting a number to binary code is a simple matter of subtraction. First, look in the chart for the biggest number equal to or less than the number you want to convert. For the number 13, this number is 8. Write a 1 in the 8 column, then subtract 8 from 13. This leaves 5. Now look for the biggest number equal to or less than 5. This is 4, so write a 1 in the 4 column, then subtract 4 from 5. This leaves 1. The number equal to or less than 1 is 1, so write a 1 in the 1 column. Write a 0 in the remaining columns. Now read the number, omitting the 0 under the 16 column: 1101.

Any number can be converted to binary code. For numbers greater than 31 (the limits of the chart shown here), just add more columns to the left, doubling each successive number (32, 64, etc.).

Sound Signals

Electrical signals travel to the different parts of your stereo through wires, but what connects a radio station to your radio? The answer is "Nothing at all." Electricity causes radio waves that travel through the air. These waves are sent from the radio station's antenna, and are picked up by the antenna in your radio set. Radio waves enable us to communicate with astronauts on the moon.

7

Reading Music

People have been writing music down since the tenth century. Before that, nobody could explain what a tune sounded like without singing it. Just like a story told before the printing press was invented, a tune probably changed a bit each time it was sung.

Rhythm Basics
• • • • •

Do you feel like clapping or dancing while listening to your favorite music? The beat is so strong, you just can't sit still. And you can clap along even if you've never heard the song before. That's the power of rhythm.

Rhythm is the timing of music. It probably stems from the most familiar rhythm of all: your heartbeat. Rhythm determines how music moves and flows. Think of the song "My Country 'Tis of Thee." If you clap along, it sounds like this: *clap*, clap, clap, *clap*; clap, clap. The first beat and every third beat after it is louder than the others, because they start the song's three-beat rhythm. When the music is written down, these three beats are placed together in a group called a **measure** or **bar**.

Native American Dancing Bells

♪ *Native Americans often wear bells while they perform their tribal dances. Put these bracelets on your ankles as you dance to the beat.*

What You'll Need

10 medium-size jingle bells (available in a crafts supply store)

two 8-inch (20-cm) pieces of ¼-inch (0.6 cm)-wide elastic (available in a fabric store)

ruler

pencil

8 sheets of colored paper

scissors

stapler

STEP 1

What to Do

1 Thread 5 of the bells onto a piece of elastic, spacing them 1½ inches (3.75 cm) apart.

2 Tie the ends of the elastic together.

3 Draw one 4-by-2-inch (10-by-5-cm) rectangle on each sheet of colored paper. Cut out each rectangle.

4 Hold one rectangle flat on the table, placing your index finger widthwise across the center of the paper. Cut fringes on one side of the paper, then turn the paper around and cut fringes on the other side, as shown.

STEP 4

5 Wrap the fringed rectangle lengthwise around the pencil. Slide the pencil out of the rolled paper.

6 Fold the rolled paper in half lengthwise, then slip it over the elastic between two bells.

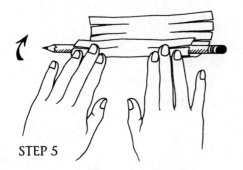

STEP 5

7 Staple the paper in place on the elastic.

8 Repeat steps 4 to 7 with the rest of the rectangles. You have made a dancing-bell ankle bracelet.

STEPS 7 AND 8

9 Repeat steps 1 to 8 to make another ankle bracelet.

Dancing Game

♪ Here's a fun game to play with a group of friends.

What You'll Need

1 set of dancing-bell ankle bracelets for each player

5 or 6 players

What to Do

1 Have each player put on bracelets, then everyone form a large circle.

2 One at a time, let someone be in the middle and dance a simple rhythmic pattern, complete with accented beats (extra-hard ankle shaking); for example, one hard shake with the right foot, followed by three soft shakes with the other foot.

3 Have everyone else dance to the rhythm, showing they can imitate it.

4 After practicing this rhythm for a while, let the dancer in the center choose the next leader.

5 Repeat until everyone gets a chance to lead the dance.

Understanding rhythm is most important when musicians play together. Everyone has to agree when to start and how fast to play. Each note has to lead to the next at the proper time to keep everyone playing together. This might be impossible without some kind of leader showing the players when to play.

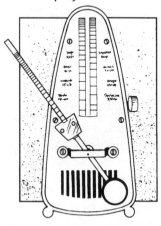

A person who leads is called a conductor. You'll learn more about this job in the next chapter. A special device, called a **metronome**, can do part of a conductor's job by clicking steadily at a given speed to mark the beats in music. With a metronome, everyone knows when they should be playing. In a recording session, bands may use something called a click track. The players wear headphones to hear clicks indicating the beats of the music. The clicks work just like a metronome.

If you have a clock that ticks out the seconds, try tapping twice or three times a second, keeping the beat steady. You'll see it takes some practice to stay right with the clock. Musicians have to listen carefully to each other to make sure they're playing at just the right time.

Music uses a simple method to indicate rhythm. **Notes** are symbols that show how long a musical sound should last. In the list shown, each succeeding note lasts twice as long as the one before.

♪ 16th note

♪ 8th

♩ quarter

♩ half

o whole

Once you recognize the symbols, you still have to know how fast to play the notes. This is very important. What would happen to a marching band if the conductor played so fast you had to run just to keep up?

This is where the metronome helps. Often you'll see a message at the top of a page of music, explaining how fast to play. Called a metronome mark, this message might read, "Quarter = 76." This means to set the metronome to 76, and play each quarter note to match the metronome's ticks.

Certain instruments are used to emphasize rhythm. A snare drum might mark out each beat in a march. A cymbal or bass drum could mark with a crash a very important point in the music. A bass guitar could play a simple tune to reinforce the rhythm in a rock band.

Rhythm Game

Here's a way to practice playing different rhythms.

What You'll Need

3 players

What to Do

1 Ask one player to tap a steady beat on a tabletop. These beats are quarter notes.

2 Listen to the player's rhythm and try to tap exactly twice as fast. These beats are eighth notes.

3 Have a third player join in. This player should tap half as fast as the first player's quarter notes by tapping one beat for every two beats the player taps. These beats are half notes.

Scratchin', Crashin' Glove Bumpers

With this instrument you can be the whole rhythm section.

What You'll Need

needle and thread (*NOTE: Please ask for help using the needle.*)

8 large buttons

old pair of gloves

4-by-2-inch (10-by-5-cm) piece of sandpaper

scissors

masking tape

ribbon

adult helper

What to Do

1 Ask an adult to help you sew the buttons on the palm side of the gloves' fingertips.

2 Fold the sandpaper in half widthwise, then cut along the fold to make two 2-inch (5-cm) squares.

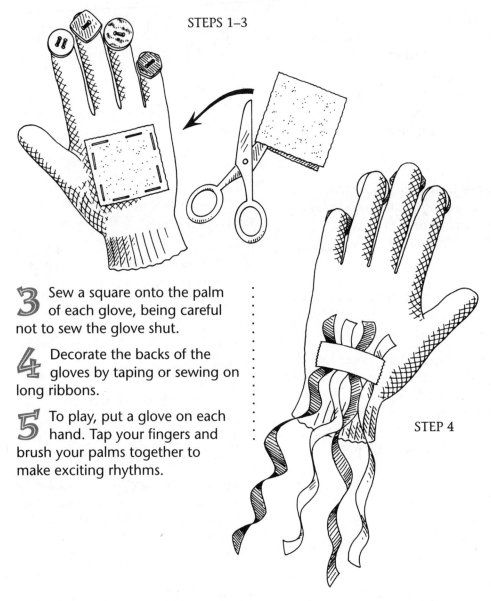

STEPS 1-3

3 Sew a square onto the palm of each glove, being careful not to sew the glove shut.

4 Decorate the backs of the gloves by taping or sewing on long ribbons.

5 To play, put a glove on each hand. Tap your fingers and brush your palms together to make exciting rhythms.

STEP 4

Scientist's Corner
Galileo's Pendulum

What affects a pendulum's swing?

What You'll Need

scissors

ruler

string

fishing sinkers, 2 of the same weight plus 1 or 2 of different weights

shower curtain rod, firmly secured

clock with second hand

paper and pencil

helper

What to Do

1 Cut the string into two lengths, one 20 inches (50 cm) long, the other 25 inches (62.5 cm) long.

2 Tie one end of each string to a sinker of the same weight.

3 Tie the other ends to the shower curtain rod so that one sinker hangs 10 inches (25 cm) from the rod and the other hangs 15 inches (37.5 cm).

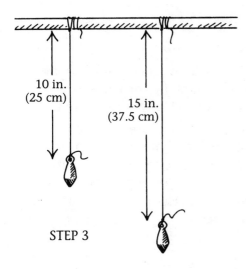

10 in. (25 cm)

15 in. (37.5 cm)

STEP 3

4 Pull one sinker back about 3 inches (7.5 cm) and release, letting it swing. Be careful not to shove it. Just let it fall away from your hand.

5 Ask your helper to use the clock to count 10 seconds while you count the number of swings that occur in that time. One swing is measured as the path the weight travels in one direction. One trip back and forth is two swings. Multiply by 6 to get the number of swings per minute. Record your results.

6 Pull the same sinker back about 2 inches (5 cm) and release. Repeat step 5.

7 Repeat steps 4 through 6 with the other sinker.

8 Repeat steps 1 through 6, using sinkers of different weights tied to the rod with identical lengths of string.

What You Discovered

For each sinker, the number of swings per minute is the same for small and larger swinging motions. Sinkers of different weights hung from equal lengths of string travel the same number of swings per minute.

GALILEO (1564–1642) was a fine musician. He played the lute (an early guitarlike instrument) and organ. He studied the construction of stringed instruments and learned how strings make musical sounds. Galileo was also very interested in astronomy. Unlike most authorities of his day, who thought the earth was at the center of the universe, Galileo believed the earth orbited (traveled in a curved path) around the sun. His interest in astronomy led to truly amazing discoveries. Viewing the night sky with a telescope he designed himself, Galileo discovered the moons of Jupiter and the rings of Saturn.

Most people have heard of Galileo and the story that he dropped weights from the Leaning Tower of Pisa, in Italy. The idea was to prove that different weights fall at the same speed. Galileo was usually very careful to write about his experiments. Because he never mentioned this one, historians have decided that he never actually did it.

Galileo did make a discovery about swinging weights called **pendulums**. While watching a heavy chandelier swinging overhead in church, he realized that small swinging movements took just as much time as larger ones. The pendulum is important for musicians as the basic principle behind the metronome, which clicks steadily at different speeds to help musicians play together.

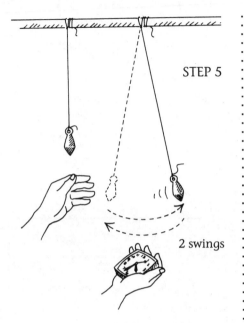

STEP 5

2 swings

Your first two pendulums swung at the following speeds:

10-inch (25-cm) string	120 swings per minute
15-inch (37.5-cm) string	96 swings per minute

Writing Down Pitches
• • • • •

Writing down music starts with five horizontal lines called a **staff**. Think of it as a ladder for the pitches to sit on. As you climb up the ladder, the pitches get higher and higher. Pitches are assigned letters from A to G.

The sign at the left of the staff is called the G clef because it indicates that the pitch G should be written on the second line from the bottom. The line names and their corresponding pitches, starting from the bottom, are E, G, B, D, and F. The space names and pitches from the bottom up are F, A, C, and E. To write down pitch C, a note is placed on the C space. Each note on the staff represents a single pitch.

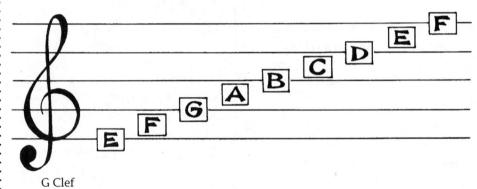

G Clef

Music Puzzle

Here's a little puzzle to help you practice reading music. Write down the letter name of each note to see if you can discover the hidden message.

Answer: I fed an egg to Dad in bed.

Reading Music with a Piano

It's easy to find the pitches on a piano keyboard.

What You'll Need

scissors
ruler
paper
marking pen
transparent tape
piano or other keyboard instrument

STEP 3

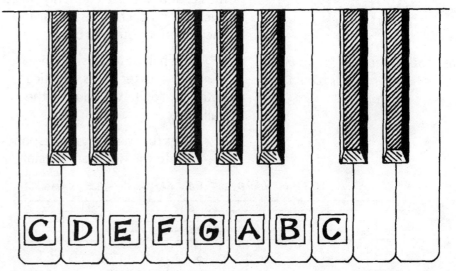

What to Do

1 Cut eight ½-inch (1.25-cm) squares of paper.

2 Label each square with a letter A through G, with two Cs as shown.

3 Tape the paper squares on the middle piano keys as shown. These are the pitches of the keys.

4 Look at the staff for "Old MacDonald Had a Farm." Press the keys that correspond to the pitches on the staff, indicated by Xs.

STEP 4

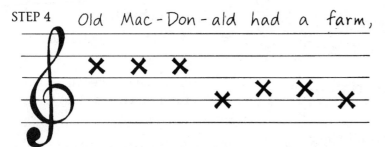

Old Mac-Don-ald had a farm,

What You Discovered

You know which keys to press by understanding that the Xs correspond to piano keys. You are able to read and play the song "Old MacDonald Had a Farm."

Playing From Real Music

Instead of Xs, the staff in this activity uses the note symbols listed on page 82.

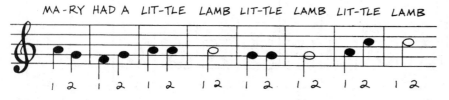

MA-RY HAD A LIT-TLE LAMB LIT-TLE LAMB LIT-TLE LAMB

1 2   1 2   1 2   1 2   1 2   1 2   1 2   1 2

What You'll Need

keyboard with letter labels from the previous experiment

What to Do

1 Notice that the staff is divided into measures with two quarter notes in each. Read the music, and practice counting "one, two" during each measure, giving each quarter note one beat.

2 The half note lasts as long as two quarter notes. Practice counting "one, two" during the half note.

3 Press the piano keys corresponding to the notes on the staff.

Musical Doorbell

Make musical notes that will play their own tune.

What You'll Need

pencil
2 sheets of construction paper
scissors
aluminum foil
ruler
3 flexible drinking straws
transparent tape
yarn
2 jingle bells (available in a crafts store)
5-by-6-inch (12.5-by-15-cm) piece of paper
color markers
glue stick
adult helper

What to Do

1 Use the pattern to draw three musical notes on a sheet of construction paper.

STEP 1

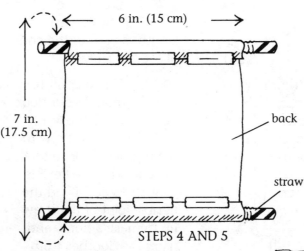

6 in. (15 cm)

7 in. (17.5 cm)

back

straw

STEPS 4 AND 5

2 Cut the notes out and cover each with foil.

3 Draw a 6-by-7-inch (15-by-17.5-cm) rectangle on the other sheet of construction paper and cut it out.

4 Wrap one 6-inch (15-cm) edge of the paper rectangle around a straw and secure with tape.

5 Wrap the opposite edge around another straw and secure with tape.

6 Tape 5 pieces of yarn of varying length to the paper along one of the edges to which a straw is attached, making the longest piece 10 inches (25 cm) long.

7 Tie the bells and tape the notes to the pieces of yarn, alternating bells and notes as shown.

8 Design your own page of music on the 5-by-6-inch (12.5-by-15-cm) piece of paper. Decorate the page with color markers. Apply glue stick to the back. Press the page onto the front side of the construction paper taped to the straws.

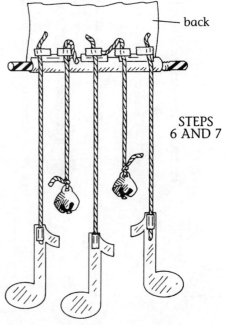

back

STEPS 6 AND 7

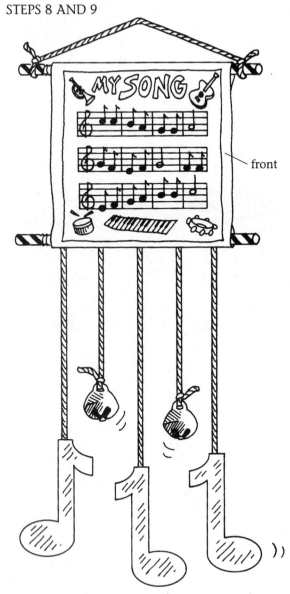

front

9 Tie the ends of an 8-inch (20-cm) length of yarn to the ends of the top straw.

10 Ask an adult to mount your doorbell by taping the long end of a flexible straw to the top of a door so that the end with the flexible joint sticks out. Bend the flexible joint of the straw up to make a hook, and hang the doorbell from the hook. The bells will jingle when you open and close the door.

8

Conducting Your Orchestra

Now that you understand a little about written music, you might wonder why professional musicians need a conductor. They are so well trained, why don't they *just know* what to do? The answer is that even the best-trained players need a conductor to show the exact timing of the music. With a hundred musicians in an orchestra, there are a hundred ideas of what proper timing is. The conductor's job is to unite the players into a team. This is easier said than done.

If you wanted to conduct, you would have to show your musicians how fast to play. You could tap quarter notes on your desk, or you could wave your arm once for each beat. When you do that, you're conducting.

Conductor's Tux

🎵🎵 *This outfit is a must for any serious conductor.*

What You'll Need

men's large white T-shirt
black felt-tipped marker
ruler
scissors
masking tape
newspaper
small sponge
bowl of water
black tempera paint

What to Do

1 Lay the T-shirt flat with the front side faceup.

2 At each side seam, make a mark 10 inches (25 cm) from the bottom. Cut along the seam from the bottom to each mark.

3 On the shirt front, find the center point along the bottom. Measure 16 inches (40 cm) from this point, and make a mark on the shirt.

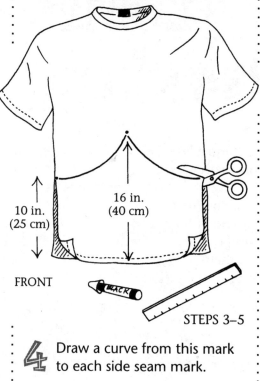

FRONT

STEPS 3–5

4 Draw a curve from this mark to each side seam mark.

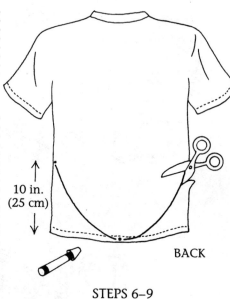

BACK

STEPS 6–9

5 Cut the front along the curves. Discard the cutaway section of the shirt.

6 Flip the shirt over and lay it flat with the back faceup.

7 Mark the center of the bottom.

8 Draw a curve from the center mark to each side at the 10-inch (25-cm) mark.

9 Cut the back along the curves.

10 Flip the shirt over and lay it flat with the front faceup.

11 From the center point marked in step 3, measure 1 inch (2.5 cm) up and make a mark.

12 From this mark, draw two straight lines, one to each side of the neck, creating a triangular area.

13 Cover this triangular area completely with masking tape.

14 Cover your work area with newspaper to protect from spills.

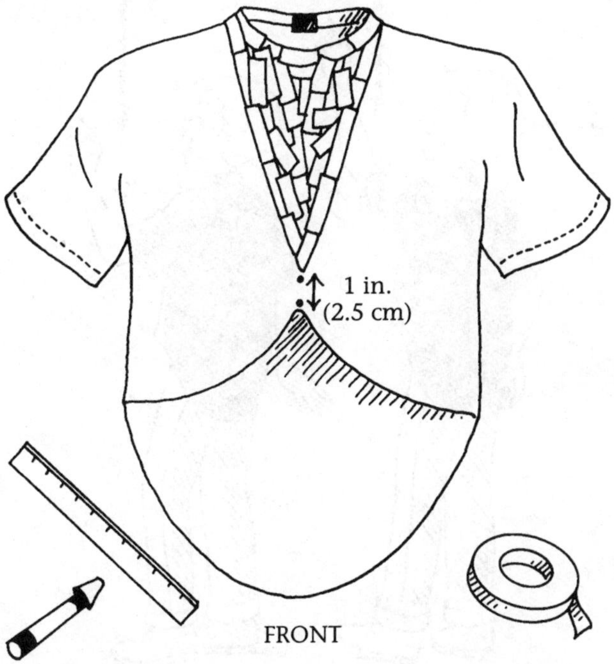

1 in. (2.5 cm)

FRONT

STEPS 11–13

15 Put a layer of newspaper inside the shirt under the triangular area.

16 Dampen the sponge with water, dip it into the paint, and gently press it over the shirt. Let the shirt dry, then turn it over and paint the back.

17 Remove the masking tape, then use the black marker to draw a bow tie.

To conduct "Mary Had A Little Lamb," imagine a big L right in front of you. Count slowly to yourself: one, two; one, two. These counts continue through the whole song. During count one, move your hand from the corner of the L, right along the bottom line, and back to the corner. During count two, your hand moves up and down the vertical line. Each count begins at the corner of the L. Practice this to make a smooth motion tracing the L.

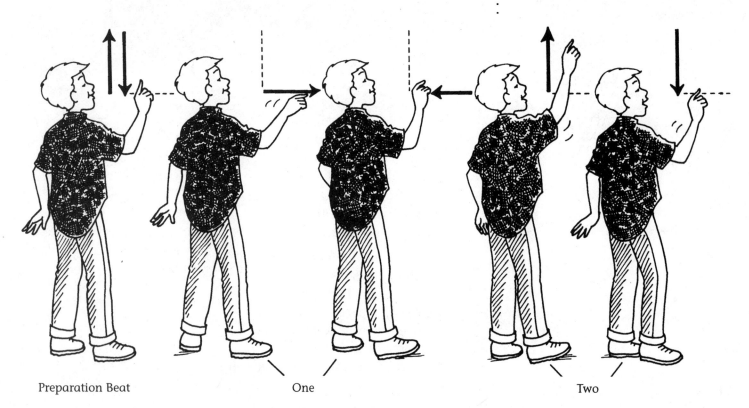

Preparation Beat   One   Two

Conducting a Song

The great moment has arrived when all your friends can play the instruments you've made. While they play one of your favorite songs, you can conduct them to make sure they play together. Some can even play solos if you'd like.

What to Do

1 Make sure your group is watching you before you start conducting. Otherwise, one player may get a head start over another.

2 Give a friendly smile as you're getting ready. You don't want anyone to think you're going to be bossy just because you're the conductor.

3 To show you're ready for the music to begin, put your right hand in front of you at about neck level.

4 Give a "preparation beat" by waving up to your forehead and back down to neck level. When your hand comes back down, this is beat one and the music starts.

5 To conduct "Mary Had A Little Lamb" (found on page 88): After a preparation beat, start beat 1. It's a right-and-left wave, corresponding to *Ma*. Swing your hand up and down the L's vertical line for the second beat, *-ry*. Continue so your hand gives a beat for each of the marked syllables.

In addition to notes, composers use words to explain how the music should sound. Starting hundreds of years ago, many composers from different countries used Italian words like the following for their explanations. Even today, some composers continue this tradition.

Forte	Play loudly.
Piano	Play softly.
Vivo	Play energetically.
Doloroso	Play sadly.
Appasionata	Play dramatically.
Presto	Play very fast.

Body Language for Conductors

During a concert, conductors can't speak to tell players what to do. Instead, they use gestures, or body language, to get their message across. They often use the right arm to show each beat and the left arm to give gestures. Each conductor has an individual style of body language. Some wave their arms around like trees in a storm. Others hardly move, which has the unintended effect of inviting the players to go to sleep. For certain effects, a conductor might use these gestures:

Arms overhead, big beats	Play loudly.
Finger to mouth like a whisper	Play softly.
Precise, smaller beat movements at chin level	Play together carefully.
Angry pointing to an individual player	Hey, wake up!
Careful pointing to a player and a signal to start	Your turn to play.

Being a good conductor is much more complicated than waving your arms. You must understand how each instrument is played and listen carefully to each part of the orchestra. For now, you can practice the beat patterns you have learned while listening to your favorite songs. Come up with body language all your own. Be as wacky as you like.

Glossary

acoustic Not electrically amplified.

amplify To make louder.

bar See **measure**.

binary number system A number system in which each number is represented as a series of zeros and ones.

bone conduction The process by which sound travels through the bones to the inner ear.

cavity A hollow space.

chord Three or more pitches sounded at the same time.

cochlea A coiled, fluid-filled tube in the inner ear that converts the eardrum's vibrations into electrical pulses and sends them to the brain.

compression wave A wave that occurs when the molecules of a material are alternately compressed and expanded.

electromagnet A coiled wire that becomes a magnet when electricity flows through it.

faun A creature of Roman mythology having the upper body of a human and the lower body of an animal.

flamenco A type of music that features rhythmic tapping of a guitar's body to accompany a dancer.

frequency The number of waves passing by in 1 second.

frets Metal ridges set into the fingerboard of a stringed instrument to show the player where to put his or her fingers.

grand piano A large piano in which the strings lie horizontally in a frame.

keyboard The name given to a group of musical instruments that are played by pressing a row of keys which, in acoustic instruments, are attached to hammers that strike strings and, in electronic instruments, are attached to external speakers and an amplifier.

lute An early guitarlike instrument.

measure A grouping of musical beats according to the music's rhythm; also called **bar**.

melody Several pitches played one after the other as a tune.

metronome A device that clicks at a given speed to mark the beats in music.

MIDI (musical instrument digital interface) A method of connecting electronic instruments to each other or to a computer.

mute   A device that fits onto an instrument and softens its sound.

note   A symbol showing how long a musical sound should last.

pendulum   A hanging weight that swings back and forth.

pitch   A name, usually a letter from A to G, designating how high or low a musical sound is; also called **frequency**.

pizzicato   By means of plucking rather than bowing.

reed   A thin piece of wood usually set in the mouthpiece of a wind instrument, which vibrates to produce the instrument's basic sound.

resonate   To vibrate along with the vibrations in the surrounding air.

rhythm   The timing of music, showing how it changes and moves.

splice   To join together cut pieces of audiotape.

staff   Five horizontal lines used to notate music, with pitches getting higher from bottom to top.

synthesizer   An electronic, usually computerized, instrument that can produce any type of sound.

tension   A condition of the strings of an instrument that is caused by stretching them taut.

upright piano   A piano in which the strings are arranged vertically.

ventriloquist   A person who can make his or her voice seem to come from somewhere other than the mouth.

vibration   A small, rapid movement that repeats itself.

wave   A regular movement traveling in a material. Light waves, however, travel through empty space.

white noise   An even blend of sound waves from the lowest frequency to the highest.

Index

electronic keyboard, 37
electronic music, 69–72
elephant, 15

F

faun, 46
Feynman, Richard, 63
fiddle, 30
flamenco, 25
flute, 41, 46–47
Franklin, Benjamin, 7
French horn, 49–50
frequency, 12
fret, 20, 25
frog, 20

G

Galileo, 85
glass harmonica, 7
gondoliers, 82
gong, 56, 65, 67
Goodman, Benny, 45
grand piano, 36
guitar, 5, 25, 83
  hollow body, 23–24
  shoe-box, 26

strings, 20
tapping body, 25

H

harmonica, 5, 7
harp, 22, 36
harpsichord, 37
hearing, 13–14
  animal, 15
  limitations, 14
  See also deafness

I

imagination game, 68

K

kettledrums. *See* timpani
keyboards, 36–37

L

Leonardo da Vinci, 68
lightning, 9
Lipscomb, William N., 45
long-playing records (LPs), 74

M

magnetic tape, 76
mallet, 64
marimba, 56
"Mary Had a Little Lamb," 88, 94,
  95
measure, 80
melody, 25
metronome, 82, 83
microphone, 74, 76
MIDI (musical instrument digital
  interface), 72
motors, 74, 76
movement, and sound, 4
musical notes. *See* notes
mute, 24

N

nature, sound in, 16–17
navigation, 11
notes, 82–83, 88–90

O

oboe, 43–44
orchestra, 91
organ, 51–53
owl, 4